# BIG POPPA E
# GREATEST HITS
## POEMS TO READ OUT LOUD

sanctum sanctorum productions
*austin • seattle • chico • wichita • bakersfield*

**big poppa e + greatest hits = poems to read out loud**
copyright 2007, eirik ott • ISBN 978-0-6151-4948-6

**email:** eirik@brokenword.org
**website:** http://www.bigpoppae.com
**journal:** http://poetryslam.livejournal.com
**online store:** http:/stores.lulu.com/poetryslam
**wikipedia entry:** http://en.wikipedia.org/wiki/Big_poppa_e
**photos:** http://www.flickr.com/photos/poetryslam
**videos:** http://www.youtube.com/poetryslam

the following poems
have been previously published
in the following chapbooks:

**the wussy boy manifesto (2002)**
the wussy boy manifesto; wallflower; jesus moshpit;
receipt found in the parking lot of the super walmart.

**missing (2002)**
roadtrippin'; chain record store blues; leaving las vegas;
poem for a friend; pushing buttons; floss; the home front;
the sweet mysteries of hot peach cobbler; immortalized in celluloid.

**exploding heart (2002)**
crushworthy; real live über grrl; poetry widow; the girl on the bus;
there's a hole in my heart in the shape of her smile that will never be filled.

**big poppa e's magic poetry (2003)**
krakatoa; the double glass doors of your heart; passersby;
sorrow, part 2; 13 metaphors for why we should've never dated.

**come destroy me (2005, 2007)**
propers; mission statement; muscleman; napoleon; tigerlily; death wish;
disillusion curry; closer to the heart; emo love song in the key of 9-3/4;
someone; open letter; oh, canadian fedex lady!

**the following poems appear here for the first time:**
the wisdom of scars; redneck; not drowning but waving;
falling in like; ode to dwarf planet 134340.

***this collection is dedicated to:***

every kid who's ever slammed poetry
or competed in a speech tournament
or simply written their own words
in a tattered notebook for only themselves to see

my family
richard and sandi and sabrina
for putting up with my nonsense for so long

my kitties aretha and thelonious
for being the most stable force in my life

marc smith
the father of poetry slamming

the genius of richard pryor
jenny holzer
barbara kruger
henry rollins
etheridge knight
david sedaris
and spaulding grey

everyone
who's let me sleep
on their couch

zara
my best friend
my habibi
my left arm

*continued on page 107...*

## table of contents

propers ......................................................................................... 1
the wisdom of scars ..................................................................... 3
mission statement ....................................................................... 6
muscleman .................................................................................. 8
¡the wussy boy manifesto! ........................................................ 11
falling in like ............................................................................. 14
ode to dwarf planet 134340 ...................................................... 17
closer to the heart ..................................................................... 20
emo love song in the key of 9-3/4 ............................................. 22
wallflower .................................................................................. 24
jesus moshpit ............................................................................. 26
napoleon .................................................................................... 27
chain record store blues ............................................................ 30
floss ........................................................................................... 32
oh! canadian fed-ex lady! .......................................................... 34
disillusion curry ......................................................................... 37
the double glass doors of your heart ........................................ 38
immortalized in celluloid ........................................................... 39
13 metaphors for why we should've never dated .................... 41
deathwish ................................................................................... 43
receipt found in the parking lot of the super walmart ............. 45
roadtrippin' ................................................................................ 48
leaving las vegas ....................................................................... 50
poem for a friend ...................................................................... 53
open letter .................................................................................. 56
pushing buttons ......................................................................... 58
krakatoa ..................................................................................... 61
the homefront ............................................................................ 64
the sweet mysteries of hot peach cobbler ................................ 68
redneck ...................................................................................... 71
poetry widow ............................................................................. 75
passersby ................................................................................... 78
the girl on the bus .................................................................... 80
sorrow, part two ........................................................................ 83
not drowning, but waving ......................................................... 85
tigerlily ...................................................................................... 87
someone .................................................................................... 88
real live über grrl ...................................................................... 90
crushworthy ............................................................................... 92
there's a hole in my heart in the shape of her smile ............... 95
notes ........................................................................................ 101

# introduction

The first time I ever heard of *slam poetry* was at an interp workshop about ten years ago. A well-known coach from the educational competition circuit in Texas stood and read something funny and poetic and engaging to us about a kid named Ernie, and I knew my life as an interp coach would never be the same again.

This was exactly what I had been looking for and not been able to find anywhere else in the world of published poetic works. He told us that it was an example of an exciting genre of poetry called *slam poetry* that he had been exposed to in a bar in New York, where poets got up and competed against each other and the patrons chose the winning interper.

I immediately thought, "Wow! A bar... WOW! This is odd and yet cool, but how could I get that sort of thing out to my kids without getting fired?" I had formerly thought of *slamming* as a way to insult people and knew that taking the kids to a bar was, without a doubt, out of the question. I had so very much to learn! Yet, I couldn't find that particular poem or anything related to it anywhere. It was like some illicit drug: What the heck was this *slam poetry* thing, and where could I get it?

The next time I heard a slam poem was later in that same season when a kid at a tournament read what I thought was possibly the funniest poem I had ever heard: *The Wussy Boy Manifesto*, by Big Poppa E. I went to Barnes and Noble on the way home, and low and behold, there was a book called *Poetry Slam: The Competitive Art of Performance Poetry*. It was, I thought, the Holy Grail of poetry: An anthology of different poems by a host of poets, both funny and poignant, lyrical and narrative, and AWESOME!

My love affair with slam poetry and the work of Eirik Ott, better known as Big Poppa E, had begun. Within the two hundred and thirty plus page book lived the one and only published poem of one Eirik Ott, aka Big Poppa E. Since then, I have heard Eirik perform at conventions, talked to him via email, absconded with a few of his self-published chapbooks, and had the privilege of hearing a number of his poems being interpreted by my own students and others throughout the state of Texas. In fact, the first time I met him, I asked about his official birthdate, due to the fact that proof of birthdate of the poet was a requirement of one of the poetry categories the kids were doing that year, and he handed me one of his expired driver's licenses, quipping, "I guess I can trust a speech teacher, what with all the identity theft going on..." Then he snatched it right back, jammed it into his wallet, pushed that into his pocket, and started quoting one of his amazing poems about his girlfriend. I stood there stunned and then mezmerized at the total transformation from ordinary guy to incredible performer.

I hope I sat down.

I love slam poetry and admire poets like Eirik and his contemporaries because they take a literary form that seems so foreign to students and adults today and transform it into something incredibly visceral and yet accessible. Think about it. Would you rather read a poem by Eirik Ott or Big Poppa E? Slam is a world where even pseudonyms are cleverly designed to gain interest.

Slam poetry, in particular, lends itself to oral interpretation because that is exactly why it was written in the first place. These guys and gals produce work that, as Taylor Mali says, "hits hard in the heart," and yet can be amazingly clear when spoken aloud. Poetry, by the very economy of words, tends to be an amazing game of word play, where readers are required to ascertain not only the written themes but also to read between the lines in a literal sense for more esoteric ideas. The great thing about spoken word poetry like slam, though, is that the speaker can communicate the thoughts, themes, and emotions in direct ways through oral presentation. Suddenly, pauses become as meaningful as sounds, and words, chosen for how they feel in your mouth, actually get to *act* how they were meant when written in the first place.

Not to sound like too much of a groupie, but I have a hard time now finding anything but slam for my interpers to compete with because slam works so well, no matter what gender, race, or creed the students are. Kids, in turn, latch on to the work of BPE and others and cultivate a love for a literary form that has formerly turned them off. Glossophobia, the fear of public speaking, gets banished because the kids feel as though words of slam poets speak for them so well that they can actually get in front of a live audience and perform with no fear (maybe a little bit of nervous energy) but definitely a true confidence they may not have enjoyed before. And let's face it, since slam poetry is, itself, a form born of competition, then it lends itself best to, well, competition. Kids become more successful and less fearful in choosing to interpret slam of all sorts.

In this anthology, Eirik has FINALLY legitimately published many of his greatest poems that were formerly available only in limited form through his chapbooks. This wonderful compilation contains much of the humor, angst, philosophy, and straight up truth of his larger collection of poetry with an added twist. He tells us all some of his best secrets to writing and performing his beloved slam poetry.

Enjoy the book. Use it as a teaching aid. Edit it where you need to for the tastes of your audiences and for the time constraints of the competitions the kids enter.

But above all, love it. I know I do.

**Aimee Kasprzyk**
*Oral Interpretation and Studies Chairperson*
*Texas Speech Communications Association*
*Member, State Prose and Poetry Advisory Committee, Texas*

# q&a with big poppa e

Q: before we get started, we need to know when were you born, because we kinda need to prove you're a living poet born in the 20th century.

A: *look on page 67 at the small print at the bottom.*

Q: cool. so, how did you get started writing poetry?

A: *there was a little coffeehouse called Matches in my hometown (bakersfield, california) back in the early part of '92, back when grunge was king and all my little hooligan friends wore thrift store corduroy jackets and were in bands and drank a lot of caffeine. inevitably, somebody started reading poetry into a microphone one night, and then someone else did, and i was there with my backpack full of journal writing, so i got up there, too. i was just awful, but everyone was just a little more awful, so it was almost like i wasn't so bad. but yeah, who am i kidding? it was pretty bad. i kept coming back and reading, and when i ran out of old stuff, i had to write new stuff, and eventually i got a little bit better. a small group of us would drive two hours south to readings in the los angeles area to get more experience performing for different crowds, and it was then that we realized most poetry at poetry readings is bloody horrible, so we didn't feel so bad when we were horrible, too. you kinda have to dare to be really bad at something for quite some time before you finally start to get any good at it.*

Q: when did you start going to poetry slams?

A: *i had been going to open mic readings in los angeles for a while, and a friend of mine named g. murray thomas mentioned that he was going to the taos poetry circus in new mexico, and he said they had something called a poetry slam, so i decided to make the drive across the desert and check it out. i found there was a whole community of slam poets spread all over the country, and they felt like i did, that poetry didn't have to be lame and boring and stupid, that it could actually be a thrilling experience that was just as entertaining as it was empowering and engaging and* genuinely moving, you know? it was like finding my lost tribe, like hagrid coming to me and telling me i was a wizard and taking me to hogwarts. my first time on a poetry slam team at the national poetry slam was in '99 as part of the san francisco team, and we ended up tying for first place out of 48 teams. the finals was in front of 3,000 people in chicago. that was probably one of the best nights of my life.

Q: where can i get more info on poetry slamming?

A: check out www.youthspeaks.org for info on an amazing organization called Youth Speaks that works with young poets. they are awesome. if you want more info on the national poetry slam community, check out the main website for poetryslam, inc., at www.poetryslaminc.org. and you can always check out my website at www.bigpoppae.com.

Q: how'd you get your stage name?

A: i can't really remember. i think someone shouted it during a performance i was doing in san francisco around '99, and the whole audience laughed. it was meant as a joke because... obviously, i am not at all what you would see in your head if you closed your eyes and tried to envision someone who called himself big poppa e, but after that first time, everyone started calling me big poppa e, even people who had known me for years. it just kinda stuck, and then i jokingly signed up as big poppa e at a slam, and that was it. since then, i have tried to get rid of it, but it never works. i like it... it makes people think i must surely look like the guy from the green mile, but i'm just this little chubby white dude who's kinda dorky and shy. i think i must have an inner big poppa. maybe we all do.

Q: do you have any advice for young poets?

i would say read and write all the time, and never leave home without a notebook and at least two pens in case one runs out. a writer writes... that's what they do, and the whole wide world is your job site, so always come to work with your tools. you wouldn't see a carpenter showing up to work without their tool belt, you know? a firefighter wouldn't show up to a burning building in cut-offs and a t-shirt and bare feet, being all, like, "what?" so write all the time, whether you make a living at it or not, and multiply that by the rest of your life, and make sure you spend your *energy telling your truth, whatever that truth might be. and don't let the haters get you down, just listen to what they have to say, use what you can, and discard the rest. and keep writing like your life depends on it, because it does. even if you don't plan on making a living at it, it's still important to document your life because if you don't, no one else will, and then it'll be like you never existed. don't ever throw anything away!*

**Q: what is a slam poet?**

*A: that is a good question. it used to be that this term was a misnomer, meaning there were no such things as slam poets, only poets who read poetry at, among other places, slams. poetry slams were originally meant as just a high-energy place to read your poetry, and everyone was invited no matter what their style. this is changing though, and a form has resulted from the format, and we call that form slam poetry for better or worse. typically, slam poetry is not just poetry, and that's the most important thing to remember. its base is in poetry, but a very performance-oriented version meant to be read out loud in front of an audience. it also incorporates elements of stand-up comedy, dramatic monologue, storytelling, theatre, dance, hip-hop, punk rock, etc. slam poetry is a mixture of all these oral forms of creative expression and it is often very, very different from poetry written strictly for the page. slam poets are people who write this way, i guess, although i don't really like the term much. slam poets perform their poetry (or whatever you want to call it) mostly at slams during competitions, but lots of them perform outside of poetry slams, too. i prefer the term performance poet, but the term slam poet is pretty much what everyone outside of the poetry slam community uses as a blanket label, so what the hell. in the end, i don't really care what you call it, as long as you feel it.*

**Q: what do you enjoy most about being a slam poet?**

*A: i don't really consider myself a slam poet since i don't really like slamming in competition anymore, but if you mean to ask what i enjoy most about writing and performing my stuff... shoot... i'd say i love writing it, and i love performing it in front of audiences. it gives me such joy to feel this burbling in my tummy that's begging to be expressed in the dead of night, then i write in a rush for as long as it takes, then edit, and edit, and edit. and that moment when i perform it, and people are feeling it, and it's obvious a connection has been made, and now conversations are being inspired by it, and people want to extend their hands and further that connection and strengthen it, and it all just flows from that point, like waves from a bomb blast, and the energy just keeps expanding, and who knows where it will go or who it will influence or in whose mouth my words will end up, in whose mind... i love being a part of that energy. poetry makes me feel alive, like I am breathing the breath of everyone in the same room at the same time, and we all exhale as one living entity, like these little doors open up in my chest and laser beams shoot out over the ocean to guide ships to safety, only they're not ships, they're people. it makes me feel sexy and sweaty and ten-foot tall and bullet-proof.*

**Q: why is performance poetry and slamming so popular lately?**

A: *we are drowning in a sea of stimulation that wants desperately to liberate money from our pocket books and leave nothing behind but a subtle feeling in the pit of our stomachs that we just got robbed. what performance poetry can give you is so much more than a $200 million movie, 40,000 watts of sound, teevees and dvds and cd. that's all passive entertainment that seeks to dull your senses and make you into a good consumer and identify yourself by which products you purchase rather than the content of your character or your actions. what slam poets do in their live shows is force you to be an active participant in what is happening. it's totally interactive. you have to think! you can't just let it all wash over you like the latest hollywood rollercoaster ride. you have to pay attention and allow your own emotions to be triggered by the words on stage, by the breath of the poet inches from your face. you have to allow yourself to be vulnerable, and that's a very human thing to be.*

**Q: what do you think about people who say that slam poetry is not really poetry, or that slam poetry doesn't work on the page?**

A: *i'd say they were missing the point because slam poetry and page poetry are two very different creative pursuits. with page poetry, you can write in so many layers that require several readings before you finally glean all the knowledge coded into the words. a page poem can be enjoyed over time as your understanding of it deepens with every reread, and that is one of the profound joys of the form. but just try to read some of those poems out loud in front of an audience. when you have exactly one shot to read a poem and have the audience either feel what you're saying in their guts or not, you have to write in a more direct, more visceral way that lends itself to performance. it's just different. you can still enjoy a slam poem on a page — i hope, since i'm putting together this collection! — but its proper place is in the mouth of a performer on a stage.*

**Q: why did you put this collection together?**

*A: i've always wanted a proper book with a perfect spine and a shiny cover, and i sorta got tired of waiting for someone else to do it for me, so i decided to do it myself. when i started compiling all the work from the past ten years that i wanted to put out there into the world once and for all, i tried to think of who i was doing it for, and without question it was the people who come to my shows, the high school and college students whose energy and enthusiasm have made my life worth living. the young people who have gathered in coffeehouses and bars and art spaces and theatres and clubs and auditoriums and classrooms and food courts for poetry. the people who have always greeted me with a smile and a wave and a hug after a long roadtrip or plane flight or some restless evening in some hotel waiting for show time to hurry up and get there so i could get on stage where i can breathe easy again. it's for them. and my parents. and for you, whoever you are, the person holding this book i might never have a chance to meet. email me and tell me what you thought, okay?*

**Q: how much rewriting did you do on your poems?**

*A: not much. i just noticed how much cursing i do in my writing, and it made me feel like i was using curse words as a crutch when there are so many perfectly good words i could use instead. i write in a very conversational tone, i think, and that mimics the way i talk in real life, and i kinda cuss way too much. it's something i need to work on. i really believe there are no such things as bad words, just certain words that are not appropriate for all occasions, and i made sure these poems could be whipped out anytime and anywhere by anyone and no one would get suspended or fired or sued for simply saying the words out loud. i never want the cuss words to get more attention than the images and ideas within the poems, so i cleaned them up and set them on their way to fend for themselves in the big old world. i hope they make you smile and write your own poems and set them free to join all the other poems out there.*

# operating instructions

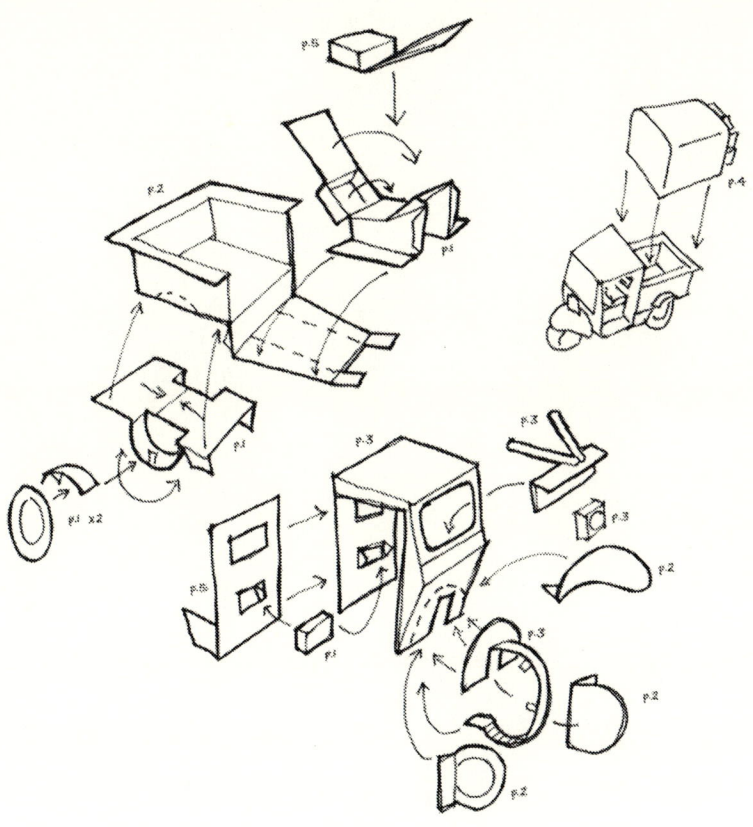

1] read these poems out loud, even if you are alone. that's what they are for. if you stifle these words with silence, they won't work nearly as well as when you breathe life into them.

2] feel free to perform these poems out loud to other people any time you like, just let them know the author's name.

3] and feel free to edit anything that might offend someone if you think that's necessary. better to take out a few things that might offend if it means the main messages and images get through.

# **propers** (2004, 2007)

this one goes out to those who refuse to be defined, who look at government forms as a challenge, who see the safe little boxes next to *caucasian* and *asian* and *black* and *hispanic* and make their own little box labelled *all of the above,* who scratch out the question entirely and write their own names in large capital letters, who, when forced to choose between *male* and *female* write instead "see attached 27-page document detailing why my gender and sexuality will never fit within the confines of your stifling need to define me."

this one goes out to those who fight every day for the simple right to exist: for every gay kid ever beaten up for being gay; for every straight kid ever beaten up for being gay; for every girl who looks into the hungry eyes of magazine models and shouts, "i don't need the body of a skinny 12-year-old boy to be beautiful! gaze at my thick thighs with envy! you can't handle the truth!"

for every boy who winces when his friends measure their masculinity by how many girls they screw over and are man enough to call them out for it. for every girl who has screamed "enough!" and marched with her sisters to *take back the night* from monsters who would rather they stay at home afraid.

for every band geek who picked up a guitar or drumsticks or a french horn instead of a bong, for every poet who picked up a pen instead of a gun and expressed their anger with words and not blood, for every jock who refused to see those physically weaker than them as less than them, and for every teacher who risked their jobs by simply being there when no one else would...

this one goes out to you.

to those who refuse to define themselves by their gpa, by the size of their parents' bank accounts, by the clothes they wear or the music

*ad-libbing is bad. follow your script.*

they listen to, to those who demand to be defined by their actions not by their fashions, who can't wait to turn 18 so they can finally vote those idiots out of office, who refuse to be passive consumers in this self-centered nation and throw away their teevees and make their own movies, who throw out their playstations and make their own videogames, who teach themselves to play their own music and write their own novels and create their own art.

and most of all... this one goes out to the kid listening right now who thinks i cannot possibly be talking about them, the quiet kid, the one who never speaks, the one with no friends, who's never been on a date, the one ignored by parents, by teachers, by other kids, yes, this one goes out to you most of all.

know this...

i understand.

i hear you.

i used to be you.

don't let anyone say your voice has no value.

raise your voice, kid, and don't ever stop.

# the wisdom of scars (2006)

*momma always told me
never look into the eyes of the sun
but momma
that's where the fun is* *

there comes a time
in everyone's life
when they must be allowed
to discover this truth:

the sweetest berries
are in the very heart
of the sticker bush.

it's the scratches
that make them sweet.

if i've learned anything
about life it's this:
a knee without scars
is evidence
of a life unlived.

children protected from playing in the dirt
grow into sick adults unable to fight
the simplest infections.

parents can't possibly redeem themselves
for past bad choices
by forcing their children
into closets

this will only make them blind
and afraid

*adolph hitler. joseph stalin. pol pot. ronald mcdonald.*

and vulnerable
and it will make them hate you.

you can't protect me
from my mistakes.
i need them.
i need the protection of callouses.
i need the wisdom of scars.

so
give me a life full of rope burns and splinters
and heartfelt advice i'm allowed to ignore.

give me shins scraped by pavement
and front teeth cracked by tree limbs
and elbows bloodied into stories worth telling.

at the end of my life
the last thing i want to see
is a long series of safe choices
and measured steps.

give me instead a life filled
with dizzying triumphs fueled
by countless lovely mess-ups
and wonderfully painful bad choices,
with cockamamie schemes that sometimes actually worked
and stories so outrageous
people never stop sharing them
as their own.

please, god, let my last dying breath
be scented with gentle regret
for foolish things i had the courage to try
and none for things i dared not do.

mistakes
are the only things

*all of your happiness is behind you.*

that have taught me anything,
and i have learned...
a whole lot.

the only lessons worth learning
are the ones that leave a mark.


\* *lyrics from bruce springsteen's* blinded by the light

## mission statement (2004)

we are poets, and that lifestyle choice may have destroyed our credit, yes, it may have destroyed relationships, yes, and it may have destroyed our backs from sleeping on couches between times when we could afford a place of our own, yes, but oh, the beauty! the soul! the whole wide world!

we live for that connection between a poet and someone moved to touch their hand to their chest and whisper "oh... i get it", between two people sitting cross-legged on dusty wooden floors bathed in joni mitchell and candlelight at 3 a.m. heads bowed hands held knees touching, between the wind and a person alone at a bus stop whispering his truth over invisible turntable breakbeats from the shady confines of his hoodie. it's all poetry — all of it! — every single breath is scented with poetry!

we will die penniless, but oh the stories! the love! the whole wide world held limp in the palms of our hands! the smiles on our faces as we bid you all goodbye with a twinkle in our eyes and so many sweet sad songs in our hearts!

so many people never get a chance to fly because they never have the courage to leap blindly stupidly floppingly out of the nest and bash themselves against all the branches all the way down, then get up and do it again and again so many times they feel like they'll die if they try again, but that's the only way to learn how to fly, and every poet who's ever spread their wings and left the bonds of this earth has a body covered in scars and bruises you feel in every word they speak.

we don't just write poetry: we live poetry. warm noses on cold windowpanes leave haiku in frost. blank pages across foreheads yield truth. we can cut our wrists on your lips and drip psalms on your tongue. we can't help it, we are poets.

people chain themselves to desks and cage themselves in cubicles and trade their precious hours on this planet for scraps of paper and a gold watch and some fleeting notion of security, and we are the crazy ones wasting time with moonbeams and seashores? we are the irresponsible one chasing fireflies and making love on rooftops?

to hell with that! poetry may be the rose-coloured glasses through which we see the world, but we get to see everything! we are not allowed to close our eyes! we do not have the right to remain silent!

we are hopelessly, painfully, ravishingly, wonderfully, terribly, horribly in love with love and life itself, even when it hurts, even when we cry and beg for it all to end, even then it's all so very beautiful and real and perfect that we carry sunshine in our chests, our ribcages cast shadows on the blind side of our skin, you can see ghosts dancing in our flesh if you squint, and we can guide ships to rocky shores just by toeing the lips of the ocean and spreading our arms wide.

our goal in life is simple: to be

wide-eyed and breathless at the wonders of the world around us and dance naked in the warm summer rain and laugh and laugh even when everything sucks because we may not always be happy and we may not always be right and we may not always be beautiful, but right here and right now we are young enough to be alive and all the stoplights are so green they sprout tendrils that tickle the tops of passing buses and the whole wide world is still so full of magic and possibility it would be an insult not to drink deeply of it.

that's what we do: we drink deeply of life in full-throated gulps.

that's who we are: we are poets.

## **muscleman** (2005)

i never wanted a weightlifter's body
bulging biceps more granite boulders than meat
carved by steel and syringes
useless
save for poses
and intimidation

no, i always wanted a swimmer's body
perfect poetry in motion
liquid made flesh
hairless and streamlined
muscles taut as drumheads
beating rhythms on the surface of the water
in a syncopated symphony of grace and power and purpose

but alas! alack!
obviously, i was graced with neither
no water has honed these thighs
no iron has etched these calves

for i...
have a poet's body

hunched-backed and pot-bellied
skin not bronzed and oiled
but pale and sallow
from basking in the radiation
of a computer screen
in a darkened room
body fueled not by steroids and energy bars
but by coffee lots of coffee lot and lots of coffee you got any coffee
where's the coffee who's got the coffee i need some freakin' coffee!

you see, this body
doesn't pump iron...
it pumps irony
into poem after poem
slinging sweat on reams
of bright white ink jet paper
and sumo-wrestling demons
by candlelight

i've traded rock hard abs
for a rock solid vocab
toned trapeziuses
for threadbare thesauruses
a mountainous gluteus maximus
for a moth-eaten moleskine notebook
and 20 reps at the bowflex
for the 20-volume set of the *oxford english language dictionary.*

oh yes, 151 pounds of pure definition!

give me a smoky poetry slam
in a dingy dive bar
over cleanin' and jerkin'
at a gold's gym anyday!

my fellow slam poets may not be muscle-bound freaks
but they are multisyllabic maniacs
lifting the masses
with the strength of their convictions
and pulling down crooked regimes
with pen strokes

my muscles propel
my fingertips across keyboards
at 86 truths per minute
and my eyes
that flick
in the direction of every sigh

and my heart
the strongest muscle in the human body
that weeps and moans and gnashes its teeth
and fights and loves so hard
it nearly bursts from my chest
every time it rains

*cameras are everywhere.*

# ¡the wussy boy manifesto! (1999, 2005)

my name is big poppa e
and i am a wussy boy.

it's taken me a long time to admit it...

i remember shouting in high school:
"no, dad, i'm not gay!
i'm just... sensitive.
i tried to like hot rods and jet planes
and football and budweiser poster girls,
but i never got the hang of it!
i don't know what's wrong with me..."

then, i saw him,
there on the silver screen,
bigger than life and unafraid
of earrings and hair dye
and rejoicing in the music
of the cure and morrissey and
siouxsie and the banshees,
talking loud and walking proud
my wussy boy icon:
duckie in *pretty in pink.*

and i realized i wasn't alone.

and now i look around
and see a whole new school of wussy boys
living large and proud of who they are:
jake gyllenhall in *donnie darko,* wussy boy!
tobie mcguire as peter parker in *spiderman,* wussy boy!
and lord god king
of the wussy boy movement:
elijah wood as frodo baggins in *the lord of the rings,* wussy boy!

unafraid to prove to all of middle earth
that two wussy hobbits
can take the dark lord down!

now i am no longer ashamed
of my wussiness, hell no,
i'm empowered by it.

when i'm at a stoplight and
some redneck testosterone
methamphetamine
jock fratboy butthead dumb jerk
pulls up beside me
blasting his trans am's stereo
with power chord anthems to big boobs
and date rape,
i no longer avoid his eyesight, hell no,
i just crank all 12 watts of my car stereo
and i rock out right into his face:
*i am human and i need to be loved
just like everybody else does!* *

i am wussy boy, hear me roar!
*meow!*

bar fight? pshaw!
you think you can take me, huh?
just because i like poetry
better than *sports illustrated?*
well, allow me to caution you,
for i'm not the average every day
run-of-the-mill wussy boy you
beat up in high school, punk,
i am wuss core!
don't make me get renaissance
on your ass because i will
write a poem about you!

*corporate sponsored rebellion is just silly.*

a poem that tears your psyche limb from limb,
that exposes your selfish insecurities,
that will wound you deeper and more severely
than knives and chains and gats and baseball bats
could ever hope to do.

you may see 65 inches of wussy boy
standing in front of you,
but my steel-toed soul is
ten foot tall and bullet proof!

bring the pain, punk,
beat the hell out of me!
show everybody in this bar
what a real    man    can do
to a smack-talking wussy boy like me!

but you'd better remember
my bruises will fade
my cuts will heal,
my scars will shrink and disappear,
but my poem
about the pitiful, small, helpless
oscar meyer weiner you really are
will last
forever!

* *lyrics from the smiths'* how soon is now

*corporations poison us with nostalgia.*

# falling in like (2007)

you make me feel... goofy.

goofy like i blush when someone mentions your name.

goofy like i have a bzillion things i wanna tell you when you're not around, but face-to-face i just stare at my toe making circles on the ground, like i'm all thumbs and no place to put them, like i just wanna write you a note that says:

*do you like me? [ ] yes   [ ] no   [ ] maybe?*

whatever random cool i've been able to harness leaps from my grasp when you enter the room, and i feel old school, and by that i mean grade school, like back in the day when the space between wanting to touch someone's hand and actually touching it could hold lifetimes of passionate yearning.

girl?

i don't wanna make out with you... i wanna make a fort with you, right in the middle of the living room with all the sheets and all the blankets and every chair in the whole house, a soft labyrinth scented with fabric softener and hot chocolate with marshmallows, laying on our tummies on the avocado shag carpeting and eating golden grahams right out of the box.

we'd be the best spellers in all the sixth grade spelling bee, and we'd spend our recesses in the library quizzing each other over dualing dictionaries and encyclopedias and having cuthroat scrabble wars, and you would always accuse me of cheating but i still swear that ISHKABIBEL is a real word, it's just not in the dictionary yet!

i would trade my grape jelly sandwich for matthew's fuji apple to switch with mikey's cherry fruit roll-up to swap with fat andy's reese's peanut butter cup — even though i am allergic to peanuts — just so i could trade your favourite candy for your grape jelly sandwich.

during art class, i would draw dr. suess landscapes of fire engine red grass and royal purple trees just so you could use the green crayon as much as you wanted.

people would talk about us... and we would let them.

and if you got the chicken pox, i would ride my bike across town on a saturday and climb in through your bedroom window to hang out with you while your parents were shopping so that i could get chicken pox, too. then we could both stay home from school and talk on the phone all day long and watch game shows and *twilight zone* reruns together and take breaks only for dinner and the bathroom until it was bed time and we whispered into the phone under the covers in the dark until we got really sleepy. and i would say, "are you asleep?" and you would say, "yesssss..." and a little while while later i would ask, "are you awake?" and you wouldn't say anything, and i would just lie there listening to the sound of your breathing.

on my homemade valentine's day card, i would write I LIKE YOU in sparkles and glue, only my handwriting is so bad, all my K's look like V's, but we decide that's better anyway... I LIVE YOU.

we'd make pinky swears while biting our thumbs and cross our hearts and hope to die promises with words like ALWAYS and FOREVER and NEVER EVER EVER, promises you can only make when you're 12 and don't know any better, back when three weeks at summer camp was an eternity and a change of schools a disaster, back before pimples, before underarm hair, before bra straps and make-up, back before graduation and college and graduation and real life, back before resumés and jobs and careers and mortgages and marriage and divorce and debt and disappointment...

back when summers... lasted... forever...

and our very first kiss... on the cheek... was the most awkward and scary and wonderful thing in the whole wide world.

that's how i like you... like... a lot.

so, which is it?

*[ ] yes*

*[ ] no*

*[ ] maybe*

# ode to dwarf planet 134340 (2006)

there are few things in this life that are strictly black or white.

most issues float somewhere in the middle of a vast sea of grey, open to a myriad conflicting interpretations.

but i am here to tell you there are such things as absolute truths, undeniable facts that rise from that wishy-washy sea of opinions and stand resolutely like venus in a clam shell for all to see.

i am talking about incontrovertible principles that are impossible to deny, of which i will now list five:

1] the sun will rise, and the sun will set;

2] all who are born will one day die;

3] van halen with david lee roth was infinitely superior to van hagar;

4] crunchy peanut butter is not only irrefutable proof of god's existence, but it also shows she loves us very much, and people who like smooth peanut butter hate the baby jesus;

and 5] which is the reason i am here right now, and i am speaking of the one remaining sterling truth no reasonable person can deny:

pluto
is a freakin' planet!

so what, a bunch of self-important professors got bored one day and decided to get back at all the cruel people who wouldn't date them in high school by knocking pluto's standing in the universe down to "dwarf planet" and renaming it 134340, and why? because pluto isn't LIKE all the other planets, pluto's SMALLER than most moons, pluto's got a bit of a STRANGE orbit, wahhhhh! but really, who in this room has never been considered an oddball? an outcast? special? let him that hath never been considered a dweeb cast the first meteoroid!

pluto is like the chubby goth girl lurking at the edge of the solar system and staring longingly at the cosmic dancefloor filled with all the popular planets... "oooh, look at me, i'm saturn, look at my freakin' rings! oooh, look at me, i'm jupiter, i'm so deep, look at my THIRD EYE!"

all these planetary john lennons and paul mccartneys vying for celestial attention while poor ringo gets pushed to the back of the universal stage.

and let me tell you... without ringo, the beatles would've amounted to nothing! ringo put the beat into the beatles, and without him, they would've just been the 'les.

without chubby goth girls, gay high school boys would never have bosoms to cry upon!

I WOULD'VE NEVER HAD BOSOMS TO CRY UPON!

pluto is the symbol for every kid who's never fit in. we need pluto as proof that no matter how small you are, how separated from mainstream society, how abnormal, how weird you are...

you, too, can be someone worth looking up to.
you, too, can be a planet.

i don't care what they say, i don't give a damn about any so-called science, forget science, this is beyond science, this is about belief, and i believe that pluto was a planet long before these bitter eggheads were mewling and puking on their mother's knees, and when they are all dead and buried along with their hoity-toity ideas and the universe has forgotten their blink of existence, pluto will still be out there...

watching over this tiny... blue... gay planet from afar like the chubby goth girl best friend it always was. call pluto what you will, but remember this...

a rose by any other name is still a freakin' planet.

*every photo you take removes you from reality.*

# closer to the heart (2005)

when i was in high school, the popular kids didn't listen to music simply because they liked it, no, the popular kids listened to music to enhance their popularity. guys didn't really like the music of journey, but the cutest girls loved journey, so if you wanted to make out when i was a sophomore, you had to at least pretend to like them.

but it didn't matter what music my friends and i listened to, because us geeks, dorks, goofs, nerds, poindexters, and neo-maxie zoom-dweebies weren't making out with anybody no matter what music we listened to, and that freed us to listen to any damn thing we wanted, and we wanted that righteous power trio from the great white north, yes, we wanted RUSH!

sure, rush was girlfriend repellent, but so were dungeons and dragons and black t-shirts with superheroes airbrushed on the front and really, really bad bacne! we weren't cool! our only possible dating partners were non-player characters! therefore, RUSH made perfect sense!

we didn't just listen to rush... we worshipped them!

rush was led by gary lee weinrib, whose yiddish grandmother pronounced his name *GEDDY,* who would grow up to be geddy lee, the best bass player in modern rock history. he was cursed with a high-pitched voice only a yiddish grandmother could love, but that voice sang of things we could whole-heartedly endorse: princes of darkness and necromancers and spaceships sucked into black holes, lords of the ring and trees that fought each other. if geddy lee could find someone to make out with him with a voice like that — and we just knew he made out any time he wanted — that meant there was hope for us, the voiceless masses who yearned to be modern day warriors with mean, mean strides of our own.

and those life-affirming lyrics were written NOT by the singer, but by the drummer, neil peart, who ensconced himself in a fortress of snares, tom-toms, double-bass, timpanis, timbales, crotales, windchimes, splash cymbals, crash cymbals, pang cymbals, and not just one cowbell... but five cowbells! when you saw rush live – which i did seventeen times between my freshman and senior year – the only thing you saw of neil peart was the spray of splintered drumsticks showering the stage like the perseid meteor shower.

and as geddy and neil laid down the beat of our pubescent hearts, alex was right there with his cherry-red doubleneck gibson guitar and camel-toed white satin pants. alex, who changed his last name from zivojinovic (zih-VAH-jen-AH-vitch) to its English translation *son of life* and became alex lifeson, whose fingertips furiously fretted six-strings and twelve-strings with surgical precision.

in our teenaged bedrooms that had never witnessed real live girls, we silenced our loneliness by cranking the best record rush ever committed to vinyl – *2112* – and wielding broomstick mic stands and singing along not just to the lyrics, but to every guitar riff, bass line, and drum fill like our sad, lonely, virginal lives depend on it.

long live rush!

# emo love song in the key of 9 3/4 (2003)

i see you sitting there in the library
with your nose pressed into a book,
and i'm sitting across from you crossing my fingers
hoping you'll stop and give me a look.

the sound of your voice makes my face go full flush,
as red as ron weasley's hair,
and i want with all of my being to reach out
and take your hand, but i do not dare.

i used to think that cho chang was the one
who was the object of my desire,
but now i know my dear you're the witch
who turns my heart into a goblet of fire.

(chorus)

*oooh oooh, hermione granger i love you,*
*i can't keep you off of my mind.*
*climb on the back of my nimbus 2000.*
*we'll leave hogwarts far behind,*
*far behind, wooo oooh oooh ooooh oooh*

sometimes i hide under my invisibility cloak
just so i can watch you from afar,
and i don't care if your parents are muggles,
the lights in your eyes shine like stars.

if i had the chance to go back to first year,
i'll tell you just what i would do,
i wouldn't take that sorting hat from my head
'till it said i belong to you.

and yeah i know *you know who* is out there somewhere
trying to kill me with his evil dark art,
but the mark he left on my forehead is nothing
compared to the lightning bolt-shaped scar on my heart.

(chorus)

i've written you a note on a scroll my dear
and tied it to my owl hedwig's leg,
and i'm hoping my words will convince you to love me,
so i don't have to fall to my knees and beg.

it says, "if you love me half as much as i love you,
meet me at midnight behind hagrid's shack,
and if you're not there i'll know that you don't,
and i'll have to find my way back to being your best friend."

(chorus)

# **wallflower** (2002)

"i can't dance!" i tell her, as i try to free my fist from the grip of this painfully beautiful woman pulling me toward the throbbing horde on the house party dance floor.

"i can't dance!"

and she purrs, "sure you can, it's easy!"

and i say, "of course, it's easy... for you! but you could be choking on a chicken bone and giving yourself the heimlich on the edge of a chair and paula abdul would be like, 'damn, that girl's got some moves!'"

but me? i hit the dance floor and epileptics come up to me and say, "brother, i know how that feels."

"i can't dance!"

what little i know about dancing i learned from molly ringwald in *the breakfast club.*

"i can't dance!"

if i kissed like i dance, i would never get a girlfriend.

*(pause)*

oh my god! i do kiss like i dance! that's why i've never had a girlfriend! but i don't tell her this, i just say, "i can't dance!"

and she fixes her feline gaze upon me and in my mind i hear her whisper, "just... watch... me."

and i am powerless to do anything but watch this goddess in the form of an english lit. major in jeans so skin-tight they are no longer fabric, they are flesh, they are a big blue tattoo with a pulse and a waistline cut so low you can almost see the baby faces of her knees peek over her belt loops.

she winks at me and wades backwards into the frothy tide of bobbing booties and begins rump-shaking this wickedly gyrating humpety-hump-hump-hump dance that defies the laws of physics, her body thrashing like a south american river full of starving piranha tearing apart an unsuspecting cow to the beat of p. diddy and missy elliot.

her blur of a behind is twitching so frantically yet so precisely she must have robotic pistons in her hips as she slips the pointy tip of her tongue to her lips. if you taped drumsticks to her undulating midriff, she'd do deadly drumrolls on the forehead of every boy on the dance floor... damn!

she's cleaving rhythmically through the booty jungle like a flesh machete, and i haven't blinked once, and she's eyeballing me, mouthing the words, "come dance with me," as she runs her open palms along the curves of her hips and quivers like a fleshy jackhammer, like a jell-o mold madonna, like a field of dragonflies fluttering their wings at once.

she's setting up sympathetic vibrations inside me like sitar strings, and my body succumbs to the rhythm, my feet shuffling, my knees bucking, my hips bumping...

then she breaks away from the crowd and walks toward me, her eyes looking all the way through me and into my beating heart that wants nothing more than for once to dance with abandon.

and the petals of her outstretched hand blossom in super slo-mo as the other dancers drip and run and fade from sight, and she gently plucks my hand and tugs me toward her, and i whisper, "i can't dance, but tonight... tonight, i'm gonna try."

*feminism is not a button on your backpack. it's a tattoo.*

# jesus moshpit (1996)

i am the biggest monster in ALL the moshpit! i don't give a DAMN and if you don't like it, i'll pull a stage dive and take your greasy punk ass out! i wade through the arching, twisting, gnashing whirlpool of elbows and knuckles, and i'll mess up ANY droog foolish enough to meet my gaze! for i am a lumbering behemoth with a six-foot tall spiked mohawk and a pierced uvula! i got arms like i-beams, fists like anvils, neck like a sewer pipe, head like a volkswagen! i shrug my mighty shoulders and sweaty punks go flying through the air like gnats off a yak's back! yea, though i mosh through the valley in the shadow of punk rock music, i shall fear NO punk! for i am the biggest, the baddest, the meanest, the no-pain-feelin'est, jack-booted-thuggin'est, steel-toe-havin'est, no-toof-grinnin'est, Boba Fett-walkin'est, Wookiee-scalp-stalkin'est punk rock monster in ALL the valley! as a matter of fact, i MADE the valley, with one mighty drag of my pinkie toe! DAMN! SHAZAAM! POETRY SLAM! GREEN EGGS & HAM! and just because you see me standing in the corner all by myself watching the moshpit mayhem from afar... skinny... in a black depeche mode t-shirt... it don't mean nothing, 'cuz i don't have to prove myself to nobody! damn!

*forests are destroyed to make room for your fat ass.*

# napoleon (2005)

it always happens.

when i rock a microphone, i feel ten foot tall and luminous, steel-toed and bulletproof, but then i'll walk triumphantly off stage and inevitably some tall idiot walks up to me and feels compelled to state the obvious:

"wow, big poppa e, you're not very big, now are you?"

well, allow me to fashion a witty retort.

TO HELL WITH ALL Y'ALL TALL PEOPLE! SHORT PEOPLE ROCK!

being short is not a shortcoming, it's a strength! all it takes to turn a tall person into a whiny little punk is a roadtrip, but me? i'm stretching out and going to sleep!

if this venue were engulfed in smoke and flames like a great white concert, all you tall people would fall to your knees trying to suck up all the good air, but us short people? we just walk right out because it's ALL good air when you're this short!

we short people are built for maximum maneuverability, dodging through crowds like liquid mercury, avoiding knees and elbows with acrobatic agility.

question: if a tall person trips and falls alone in the forest, would there be a sound?

answer: hell's yeah, there'd be a sound!

but me? i'm already so low to the ground that falling is like laying my head on a pillow. and i never bump my head on ANYTHING! if i bump my head on something, that stuff is too freakin' low!

and don't talk to me about reaching stuff, oh hell no, that's why the good lord invented chairs and tall people. "yo, michael jordan, get me that tuna can off the top shelf now!"

tall people are up to no good! all the truly innovative thinkers of the modern age have been short:

einstein? 5'3"
ghandi? 5'2"
tori amos? 5'1"
shigeru miyamoto,
the creative genius behind *donkey kong*
and *super mario brothers?*
4-foot freakin' 9!

now, i don't want you to think that i'm drinking haterade... that's not what i'm all about, with me it's all love love...

to hell with tall people!

to hell with tall people
who stand in front of you
at concerts and movies!

to hell with tall people
who take up the whole damn bed
like they own it!

to hell with tetherball!
i freakin' hate tetherball!
whoever invented tetherball is a jackass!

and to hell with basketball, too! the only good thing about basketball is that the nba has corralled those who will be shot first! oh yes, the revolution is indeed coming! and the revolution will not be super-sized, it will be minimized! and when the short people of this world unite and rise up, you might not be able to tell...

*friends don't let friends grow up.*

right away...

but when steel-toed boot shaped bruises appear on long-assed shins the world over, you will know that me, gary coleman, that kid from *webster,* and mini-me and the oompa loompas and prince have finally had enough of your crap and have begun taking over the world one step-stool at a time!

represent!

# chain record store blues (1998, 2007)

i worked at a chain record store over the holiday season and the worst thing about it wasn't the customers or the crappy hours or the crappy wages or the frenzied display of rampant consumerism posing as some quasi-religious celebration nor was it the snot-nosed kids working there who referred to me as Pops because my hair's not blue and my eyebrow doesn't have 47 piercings and oh stupid me i just bought the first spice girls album on my employee discount oh stupid me i'm not down i'm not cool i'm not def i'm not fresh i'm not phat i'm not fly i'm not old school i'm not punk rock! no, the worst thing about it was the music, man, having to listen to stupid christmas music every stupid day between halloween and new year's, and oh my god did i wanna roast nat king cole's chestnuts over an open fire! anyway, it's the afternoon of christmas eve, and my chain record store is packed with last minute shoppers, and i'm on the edge, man, after not having had a break in five hours and we're running full blast with all five registers ringing up long lines of idiots and each one of them has got a handful of screaming kids yelling "i want britney spears!" and "i want justin timberlake!" and "no, mom, eminem doesn't have any cussing on it, i promise, just buy it for me, you stupid filthy cow!" and in the middle of all this christmas joy comes this wide-eyed waif of a girl in a red babydoll shirt and baggy skater pants with seven silver hoops in one ear and a pierced lip and a pierced tongue and three nose piercings and a pierced belly button and the *star wars* rebel alliance symbol tattooed on her neck, and she wafts up to my cash register and delicately places a brand new shiny copy of christina aguilera's latest CD on my counter and says, "hi, i'm Nikkii with two K's and three I's, how are you?" and i say, "well, trish, i'll tell you, i was just thinking about having my tongue amputated and re-attached to my forehead so i can lick my own eyebrows straight! no, better yet, i'm gonna take a razor and slice my tongue in half down the middle from the tip all the way back to the uvula then i'm gonna slice it in fourths and then i'm gonna pierce the tips of each piece and attach them with silver chains to my ears so my tongue will blossom like a flower and then i'll really be punk rock don't you think that would be punk rock and i'm not gonna stop there, no, i'm gonna take body modification to a whole new level, trish!" and as i'm saying this i jump up on the counter and kick the avril lavigne display and send cds raining down onto the heads of the frightened crowd of shoppers just as the mormon tabernacle choir sings "it's beginning to look a lot like christmas" and i scream "there is no santa claus! there is no easter bunny! there's only me, and i ain't givin' you nothing!" then Nikkii with two K's and three I's says, "do you take checks?" and all of a sudden i'm back at my register behind the counter just staring at this skater chick so i say, "you know, skater chick, that christina aguilera cd sucks except for that one song on the radio," and she says, "well, it doesn't matter, it's only for my brother and he's lucky he's even getting this, so just ring me the hell up!" so i ring her the hell up and say, "have a very merry christmas, nikkii. next?"

# floss (1994)

i like to floss my teeth.

i mean, i really like to floss my teeth. there's nothing better than unwinding a good yard of floss at the end of the day, kicking back on your futon couch with your beat feet thrown over the armrest, your eyes closed, head back, listening to some Ella or Bessie or Billie or Fats on the stereo, and stretching that waxed dental floss between your fingers.

and none of that fancy stuff, none of that high-tech, space shuttle floss, and no cinnamon or mint flavoring either, just the classic type... not too thick, but just right. and you've got to pull it tight, nice and tight, nice and purple-fingertip-tight. and the music is playing and your eyes are closed and ohh... you slip the floss in between your teeth, just ease it in and scrape gently up and down along either side of your tooth, and ohhh... the pressure of a day's work just disappears, even as you remove bits of chicken chow mein and polska kielbasa sausage and strings of lemon grass and bean sprouts.

oh, it's heavenly... the pressure on your teeth, on the spaces between your teeth, just vanishes, and the sins of the day just vanish, and the missed opportunities and the relationships that never work and flesh eating bacteria and dying children in afghanistan and biological warfare in america and the world trade center and the pentagon and jihad and fatwa and holes in the ozone and the fate of the planet and what happens when you die and whether or not there's a god... it all fades away as the slender thread dances between your teeth and skitters along your gums and removes all the dreck it finds.

just to run your tongue across that pearly expanse of enamel and not find one single foreign substance, not a single unplanned particle or rebellious crumb, just smooth ivory smoothness, your tongue ice skating over the expanse of white...

i have this recurring dream. i won't tell you all about it, but britney spears is in it and we floss each other's teeth on a black leather couch with one red pillow. this dream took a strange turn the other night; instead of britney, it was my mother and she had this enormous ball of floss and it was like she was Mom of the Undead and... i woke up, suddenly, frightened by what it could mean.

mmmm, floss.

in heaven, just as you get off the elevator and still have songs of the beatles in your head, the host angel who greets you and takes you to the correct line that you'll be standing in for the next two thousand years will hand you a little white dispenser of waxed dental floss that never frays, never breaks, and never runs out.

knowing that, what in this life is impossible to take?

## oh! canadian fedex lady! (2005)

oh! canadian fedex lady!
the way you giggled
when you caught me beat-boxing
to your hold music
after you tracked my customer's package
made me want to forever renounce
my american citizenship
and emigrate to the great white north!

oh! canadian fedex lady!

if you are half as cute
as the entire city
of vancouver, british columbia, seemed
the last time i toured through canada,
then you are so very, very cute,
especially if you are also short
and wear cat's eye glasses
because short cute girls who wear cat's eye glasses
totally kick my ass!

oh! canadian fedex lady!

the fact that you mentioned
how cool it was that bob marley's *buffalo soldier*
was playing on my hold music
when i had to talk to my stupid american customer —
who was rude and mean, as most american customers tend to be,
unlike most canadian customers,
who seem every bit as polite as you —
well, that makes me think *you* are cool, too,
because i like bob marley!
only i hope you don't like bob marley too much,
as in not enough to be a smelly, nasty, hippie who also likes

*he hasn't thought about you in a long time.*

crappy jam bands like moe and leftover salmon and phish... and...
and... phish...

oh! canadian fedex lady!

i loved that you said *zed*
for the last letter in the alphabet,
and i loved how you ended most of your questions with "eh?"
and i loved that you asked me for my customer's postal code,
then giggled and apologized and said,
"oh, duh, you guys say, *'zip code,'* eh?"

and i imagine when you said that
you shyly tucked your long hair behind your ear
and rolled your big anime eyes,
and i'll bet those eyes were as blue
as the great hudson bay
only deeper
and warm.
or, better yet, green
as calgary bluegrass
in the summertime
only they wouldn't make me sneeze.
or hazel with little yellow flecks orbiting your irises like
the lights of toronto winking from the surface
of lake ontario.
and even if your eyes are brown —
like mine,
and i hate mine,
canadian fedex lady —
i'll bet they'd be the loveliest shade of brown since...

*(pause)*

pudding...
and i love pudding!

oh! canadian fedex lady!

*hear that? they're laughing at you again.*

i love rush! i love neil young! i love joni mitchell!
i love... uhm... canadian bacon...
although you probably just call it *bacon*...
unless you're a vegetarian,
in which case to hell with bacon! stupid bacon!

oh! canadian fedex lady!

i wish i had given you my website
so you could check out my poetry
and see that i am witty and i am charming
and i have tremendous taste in books, movies, and music.

and we could've used your employee discount
to send each other mixed cds for free
that would've made us fall crazy in love with each other,
and the next time i was in canada
we could've met in a cafe
and gazed lovingly into each other's pudding brown eyes
as bob marley played
over the coffeehouse stereo system
and we held hands
and smiled
and sighed.

but i didn't, and now...

i will never, ever meet you,
canadian fedex lady!
and i will never know
what colour your eyes are
when it rains,
or what you think of this poem
i just wrote for you
five minutes after we finished our call
as i kept my stupid, rude, mean american customer
on hold the entire time.

*heroin. vicadin. novacaine. love.*

# **disillusion curry** (2003)

i knew a girl once.

i don't remember her name. i may never have known her name, to be honest, but she was *the cute girl at the thai place* for a long time, my favourite waitress in my favourite restaurant in my favourite little college town.

she always made me smile.

one day, she was wearing a sheer white shirt, and you could peek right through her sleeve and see the large tattoo on her forearm. i asked her about it, and she rolled up her sleeve and showed it to me, this huge colorful tattoo... of a pepsi can...

i was... well... sort of taken aback.

i asked her about it, and she said, "yeah, i used to love pepsi. drank it all the time, so much that all my friends used to call me *pepsi*."

we paused for a moment... then i asked her about the use of the past tense, and she said, "yeah, the real shame of it is that i don't even drink pepsi anymore. i drink dr. pepper."

at that very moment, precisely as she finished that sentence, i fell deeply out of love with the cute girl at the thai place.

# the double glass doors of your heart (2003)

if you had a full-body tattoo of a 7-11 sign, i would open the double glass doors of your heart and walk inside, saunter over to the slurpee machine of love and get myself a nice 32-ounce Coke Slurpee of Faith and Devotion, then i'd sashay over to the candy aisle and get myself a nice Jumbo Butterfinger of Passion, and then i would traipse over to the magazine rack and get a fresh copy of *Juggs Magazine* of Eternity, then i would wait in line behind the guy buying a money order to pay to have his phone reconnected — and i would wonder... how that guy got in here because what the hell? this is not just some 7-11 down the block from where you live, oh no, this is the 7-11 of your soul tattooed on your body, so why the hell are you letting people in here to buy money orders? but then the guy would be done, and i would prick my finger and pay for my Coke Slurpee of Faith and Devotion and my Jumbo Butterfinger of Passion and my *Juggs Magazine* of Eternity with drops of my lifeblood, and i would make my way for the double glass doors of your heart, but the doors would be locked. and then it would occur to me that you had tricked me, you would've had that body-sized tattoo of the 7-11 sign removed with lazer technology while i was in there spilling blood for my Coke Slurpee of Faith and Devotion and my Jumbo Butterfinger of Passion and my copy of *Juggs Magazine* of Eternity — was it the *Juggs Magazine* of Eternity? i can put it back! i can get, like, *newsweek!* — and then i would just sit there, propped against the locked double glass doors of your heart, eating my Jumbo Butterfinger of Passion, drinking my Coke Slurpee of Faith and Devotion, reading my blood-stained *Juggs Magazine* of Eternity and wondering... just how long... has the counter guy been here! what the hell? do you let anyone, like, live here? in your heart? was he trapped, too, back when you had a body-sized tattoo of, what? zippy mart? is that what your heart is? a revolving door in the zippy mart of doom?

loving you is like a really weird dream
i don't even know i'm having.

*if life gives you lemons, squeeze lemon juice in its stupid eye.*

# **immortalized in celluloid** (1998, 2007)

i want a soundtrack to play at certain important parts of my life so that i'll know they're important. if i hold someone's hand and wonderful glorious choirs and a symphony orchestra kick in, i'll know it's true love. if wierd scary music plays as i walk into my dark and lonely apartment... alone... i'll know it's time to find a new place to live. if there is no music, i'll know what is happening is not very important; DMVs and post offices are places with no soundtracks... unless you're very unlucky.

i want to run down the street as fast as i can... in slow-mo... with buildings exploding and plate glass windows shattering and cars crashing and women and children screaming and bullets ricochetting and sirens blaring and lots of mayhem and destruction... then... i want everything... back to normal. and no one gets hurt. it just looks really freaking cool.

i want people to hear my deep meaningful thoughts in a whispery voice-over when i'm thinking deep meaningful thoughts so i won't have to actually tell them what's on my mind, they'll just know. when i want someone to know i am being sincere, i want my face to completely fill that person's vision so they can see i'm sincere.

i want to fast forward through the parts of my life i don't like, and when the good parts come, i want to hit *pause.* no, even better... i want to do something over and over and over again until i get it right, and i want the cutting room floor to be littered with break-ups and arguments and embarassments and speeding tickets and crying jags and sicknesses and vomiting, leaving only first kisses, paydays, sunsets, awards ceremonies, graduations, promotions, and lots and lots of passionate lovemaking.

i want a talented team of writers to script everything i say so i always say exactly what i'm supposed to say at exactly the right moment. i want all my dialogue to be lifted from the text of best-sellers and hit broadway plays. i want all my love scenes choreographed and lit by a host of talented technicans who know how to make it all look... just... right. and let me tell you, it takes a whole lot of freakin' talent to make a short, dumpy, bald kid like me look just... right...

music, of course, will be playing during these times — regina spektor... joanna newsom... ani difranco... — music that enhances the love i feel inside for this person, whose inner voice i'll be able to hear as we make soft focus love.

i want my life to be lightweight and romantic and crowd-pleasing. i want all the loose ends tied up by last ten minutes. i want my performance to appear effortless.

i want a happy ending.

# 13 metaphors for why we should've never dated (2002, 2007)

you are the jagged rusty tip of a nail sticking out of a polished
wooden banister, and i am the little kid sliding down that bannister
in baby blue felt pajamas.

you are the computer hard drive grinding to a complete halt,
and i am the last 200 pages of the great american novel
written in a mad 12-hour rush that were never saved.

you are the speeding train hurtling toward the stalled greyhound,
and i am the cure for cancer whispered by the bus driver
seconds before impact.

you are the answering machine that eats the tape,
and i am the telephone call from the lottery saying
i have just won 26 million dollars
if i just call back right... now...

you are a small furry rodent wrapped tightly in duct tape,
and i am richard gere.

you are the bullet, and i am the kennedy.

you are rock, and i am scissors.
you are scissors, and i am paper.
you are paper, and i am rock.

you are gollum, and i am frodo's ring finger.

you are a daytime emmy award, and i am susan lucci.

you are a ham sandwich, and i am mama cass.

you are a super tanker bulging with oil, and i am alaska.

you are george w. bush, and i am alaska.

you are *the matrix revolutions,*
and i am the kid from cleveland sick with cancer
who begged the make-a-wish foundation for a chance
to see the last *matrix* movie before he died
and whose last words were, "i want my stupid wish back!"

you are the dog that ate the cat that ate the rat that had the flea that
bit me and gave me the bubonic plague.

you are the curse on rock stars whose names began with *j,* and i am
jeff buckley, jerry garcia, janis joplin, jimi hendrix, jim morrison,
john lennon, john bonham, john belushi, jim croce, brian jones,
and jesus christ.

you are michael jackson...
and i am not gonna go there.

you are the sharpened spine of a sting ray's tail,
and i am *the crocodile hunter!*
and yes, i went there!

you are the proposed sequel to *the goonies*
and i am corey feldman...
waiting...
for that phone call...
for the last 20 years.

which is to say, you and i do not go together like peas and carrots;
we go together like candy apples and razor blades.

and i am aware of this... i know this... and yet...
at three in the morning,
i find myself staring at the ceiling
and thinking
about you.

*it doesn't get any better than this.*

# death wish (1999)

we are all going to die someday.

and we all have to deal with this fact our own way.

some people are new agey about their deaths, requesting that their bodies be burned in a big tibetan ceremony until their heads burst open and release their spirits skyward. then, a small gathering of friends can mix their ashes with potting soil and have a tree-planting shindig where everyone wears party hats and tells dirty stories and feels a whole lot better afterwards knowing their fallen comrade's essence was coursing through the veins of a living tree.

well, that scenario is all fine and good, but i see a slightly different scenario for my death.

call me grandiose, but when i die, i want world markets to collapse, tectonic plates to shift, volcanos to erupt, hurricanes to blow, jet planes packed with passengers to plummet from the sky, endangered species to fall dead, mountains to crumble, and the entire Bush Family to spontaneously combust the very moment i breathe my last breath.

i want virgins sacrificed by the busload and lots of weeping and moaning and gnashing of teeth when i die, and i want the thousand years following my death designated as *The Millennium of Mourning*. i want the year i was born changed to *The Year Things Got Cool*.

i want my last words to contain the cure for aids, cancer, heart disease, bad breath and the common cold and the exact location of jimmy hoffa's body. i want my crappy hometown of bakersfield, california, consumed by a holy firestorm and anyone looking at it to be turned into a pillar of salt.

*it doesn't matter what you want. do what you are told.*

i want everyone who believes in god to tear at their eyes and jump off bridges and tall buildings, and i want everyone who doesn't believe in god to make me their deity. i want the members of christian youth groups to wear little motivational bracelets that say *WWBPED* and when they look at those bracelets in times of moral dilemma, i want it to give them the motivation to launch tri-state crime sprees because that's exactly what big poppa e would do.

i want hundreds of thousands of women to claim i was the father of their love children... because I WAS the father of their love children! i want every person on this entire planet to simultaneously write in their online journal, "oh no, big poppa e died."

i want the oceans to dry up and every crop to turn brown and every puppy to get hit by a car and every voice raised in one colossal global wail.

i want obi-wan kenobi to pause, put his fingertips to his temples, stagger and say, "i just felt a terrible disturbance in the force, as if millions of voices cried out, then were suddenly silenced."

i want reality to come to a screeching halt when i die, and the only way you're gonna prevent the Apocalypse from dancing down main street in a tight red dress is by protecting me like the freakin' crown jewels because if anything happens to me, man, i am taking every one of you with me!

# receipt found in the parking lot of super walmart (2001)

soap
shampoo
hair conditioner
toothpaste
dental floss
shaving cream
after shave lotion
deodorant
hair gel
spray starch
anniversary hallmark card
flowers
candles
matches
incense
2 filet mignon steaks
2 portabello mushrooms
1 loaf sourdough bread
butter
garlic spread
paprika
fresh parsley
4 yukon gold potatoes
sour cream
fresh leaf spinach
croutons
red onions
red peppers
feta cheese
sun-dried tomatoes
slivered almonds
balsamic vinegar
extra virgin olive oil

*it's all that cashier's fault. be rude to them.*

fresh strawberries
block of white chocolate
bottle of white wine
barry white's greatest hits cd
4 aromatherapy candles
aromatherapy bath salts
aromatherapy massage oil
mr. happy back massager
hershey's chocolate syrup
honey
box of condoms, 32-count, extra large
spermicidal foam
astro glide personal lubricant
box of dental dams, 32-count, cherry flavoured
feather duster
dog leash
dog collar
fly swatter
rope
rubber gloves
hot water bottle w/ hose
clothes pins
needles
nail file
ice pick
hacksaw
plastic garbage bags, extra large, heavy duty
5 bungie cords
leather gloves, black
turtle neck sweater, black
jeans, black
knit beanie, black
hiking boots, dark brown
flashlight
d-cell batteries, 8-pack
wheelbarrow, large
shovel
black and decker mini-vac

plug-in air freshener
stain remover, heavy duty
ajax tub and tile cleaner
carpet fresh, lilac scent
bleach
scrub brush
pumice stone
5-pack sponges
2 large beach towels
1 hustler magazine
1 penthouse magazine
1 barely legal magazine
1 box kleenex tissue, deep forest series
tylenol caplets, extra strength, 128-count
melatonin, one bottle, 64-count
1 packet razor blades, 6-count
cat food

# roadtrippin' (1996, 2007)

there's something magical and healing about a solo roadtrip.

it's about forward motion, something about going somewhere and leaving something behind. it's about yearning to blow off your job, quit your girlfriend, sell off all your stuff and pack what's left into the back of your pickup truck.

it's about whittling your existence down to its necessary parts — just you, an 80-gig ipod, and a sleeping bag in the back — and throwing the map out the window and getting the hell outta Dodge.

it's about raising your head from the keyboard attached to a computer on a desk in a cubicle in a work center in a business that makes things for other businesses that sell things to other businesses and realizing that your paragraph in the Great American Novel is due for yet another rewrite.

it's about yearning to tattoo the sticky black ink of your tires across the belly of this land, to become another steel corpuscle in the freeway bloodstream and flow into towns you've never seen and follow the pulse to its beating heart.

it's about blazing down the highway, just you and patsy cline, just you and johnny cash, just you and soft cell and singing at the top of your lungs, "don't touch me please i cannot stand the way you TEASE!" at 75-85-95 miles per hour. *

it's about playing *ski-rack or cop car* for 600 miles at a time.

it's about pulling over recklessly, immediately, across four lanes of traffic to stop under an overpass to scribble a phrase or two that falls in your path like a safe from the sky.

*48*
*labels are absolutely necessary.*

it's about leaving everything behind and cleansing yourself in a gritty, sweaty, unwashed catharsis of road dirt and sunburnt forearms and parking in a field infested with crickets in some town somewhere and drifting off to sleep in the same cut-offs and radiohead t-shirt you've been wearing since diving into the colorado river in needles, california, three days before.

it's about the random encounters in gas stations and greasy spoons, in coffeeshops and dark saloons. it's about being embraced by serendipity and spirited away from the real deal angst machine of modern day existence.

it's about smiling that healing smile that only days and days on the road can bring.

i love a good roadtrip, man, that shakes your head and clears out the cobwebs and allows you to think clearly for the first time in years.

* *lyrics from soft cell's* tainted love

# leaving las vegas (1999, 2007)

i exist
in a forest of chain stores and pavement
of billboard whores and sacraments of
plastic coins and dice meant
to distract the masses from their
dreary daily routines
as wobbly cogs in the great white machine.

i exist
in an x-rated cacophony of pre-packaged destiny,
of come-hither eyes from a thousand blinding signs,
of cocktail waitresses bound in tight poly plumage
and gagged by patriarchy gone mad mad mad,
of sex-store dollar booths satiating salivating sociopaths
with eye candy debutantes and
gaily coloured tissue boxes while
minimum wage mop jockeys wait
to sop up their discarded sickness,
of oxygen mask octogenarians chain-smoking Lucky Strikes
and shuffling 'cross casino carpets
clutching change cups to skinny chests
like drowning men in life preservers,
of shipwrecked showgirls and their silicon come-ons
shaking their money maker
for drooling fools and their Viagra-choked tools
who think this must surely be the American Dream...

i exist
but i do not live
for this life is not for me
not this quagmire of consumerism
not this miasma of materialism
not this bloated corpse of sexism
this wretched hive of scum and villainy.

i see with my naked eye
fields of hunched shoulders pressed
against huge banks of slots,
rocking unconsciously back and forth
and mumbling,
stuffing quarters into slots and
coaxing their dreams to life
at the amazing Technicolor Wailing Wall.

i exist
as a shadow cast
on a casino wall
watching

sick to my soul

and yearning to leave this shopping mall town
and its chopping block people
and escape...

but where?

to a corporate culture that trades billions of pink Grandmas in
for trillions of nicotine tainted coffin-nails
and the bright, white image of the Marlboro man
called *Progress?*

to a soft drink youth movement of mass-marketed rebellion
that teaches our children to pay for their advertising
and display their logos proudly across their pubescent chests
and define themselves
not by their actions
but by their fashions?

to a sound-bite government of photo op polemics
smiling for the camera and regurgitating
the latest cross-referenced trends and poll statistics
as they kiss white babies

*lust is more efficient than love.*

and bomb brown babies
over there
somewhere?

to a society
where the term *work ethic*
means working your life away
for ethics-free companies
and *religion* means
you'll be rewarded for your sad lonely life
after you die
bitter
burnt
heartbroken
and alone?

there is no escape...

there is no leaving Las Vegas...

every town in America is Las Vegas
and we are all hopeless gamblers
on an extended losing streak
just rolling those dice
as the skyscrapers come tumbling down around us...

## poem for a friend (1999)

i imagine myself
with you, my friend,
on childhood streetcorners
sweating
in the summertime sun
sucking on frozen kool aid in a dixie cup
in the curbside shade
of a broken down pickup truck.

i imagine us
locking and popping
to old school hip hop
like boogaloo shrimp
trying to pimp
the candystore hotties
with our portable cardboard dancefloors.
we'd spin our gangly bodies
into b-boy oblivion
boombox blastin'
staccato breakbeats
while melle mel bellowed,
*don't push me 'cuz i'm close to the edge...\**
and i'd be right there with you, man,
frontin' with some white kid cabbage patch
running man mime routine
waiting for the inevitable bidding war for our music.

sucker mc's could not fade us
'cuz we was lyrical assassinators
cold cut commentators
gesticulating wildly
over plates of your great aunt's
red beans and green tomatoes
collard greens and mashed potatoes...

*pandora was a scapegoat.*

and i'm telling my friend about this dope poem
i'm writing about him and me when we was kids
and i look to him for that glowing smile of recognition
expecting imagined stories to fall from his tongue like ripe plums
populated with characters named *skillethead* and *june bug*
prefacing everything with,
"man, you remember that one time?"
and i'd say, "man, that was off the hook!"

but he doesn't smile
he just clucks his tongue
and says, "i appreciate the enthusiasm
with which you embrace
what you think
is my culture

but i have news for you, my friend —

my mother wasn't weezie jefferson
and my father wasn't fred sanford
and i didn't spend my childhood
on streetcorners
with fat albert and the cosby kids.

i don't appreciate you re-writing my childhood
so you can pretend you had a black friend.

i've lost track
of the white friends
who think *negro* is an esoteric culture
with secret handshakes and code words
you can just pick up through osmosis
through the beastie boys and blaxpoitation flicks.

it's cool you know so much
about langston hughes and
etheridge knight and
maya angelou

and it's cool you know so much
about miles davis and
john coltrane and
thelonious monk...

but that does not mean
you know anything
about me,
now why don't you go write a poem about that?"


*lyrics from grandmaster flash and the furious five's* the message

# open letter (2004)

open letter to the straight, white, middle-class, american, male poetry slammer who complained with a straight face that he is, in fact, one of the most oppressed persons in the scene because he isn't allow to, and i quote, "pull the race card."

subtitled: *twenty reasons why you should shut the hell up*

you can walk into any drug store in america and find flesh-coloured band-aids that actually match your flesh colour.

you can go to any city and be stopped by a police officer and be reasonably sure your skin color had nothing to do with it.

you can be a student at any university and not be told the only reason you are there is to fill some kind of quota.

you can be fairly certain that the neighborhood where most of the people who look like you live will not be given a cute nickname like *little montana* or *oklahoma town* or *the ghetto*.

you can do well in a challenging situation and not be called a *credit to your race*.

no one is ever going to preface a question with a phrase like, "as a straight, white, middle-class american male, what do you think about..."

no one will ever say, "you are so well-spoken... for a straight, white, middle-class american male."

no one will ever claim to have friends that look like you in order to prove they are open-minded.

no one will try to gain your approval by saying, "i love straight, white, middle-class american male food! i eat it all the time!"

no one will ever try to date you simply because you are *exotic*.

you can write about any messed up thing that's ever happened to you, and no one will ever accuse you of *pulling the race card*.

no one will ever pluck the creative fruits of your artistic labour and those of your culture then take credit for their creation and make more money from them than those who created them.

you can be sure no one will ever claim you deserved to be sexually harassed or beaten or raped because of the clothes you wear or how many people you have had sex with.

being a straight, white, middle-class american male ensures that you will probably never have to endure laws passed to prevent you from exercising your reproductive freedom and the freedom to marry someone you love, it means you have probably had more access to a higher quality of education, better housing, better health care, better police protection, better fire protection, less air pollution, less water pollution, less crime, and more political representation than any other group in the history of the planet.

if you refuse to admit your overwhelming privilege and how that privilege has helped you in this country, then how in the world can you use that privilege to change this country? and if you are not using your privilege, if you can't even admit to that privilege, then you are not just part of the problem, you ARE the problem, and until you are ready to do something about it, please just shut the hell up!

## **pushing buttons** (2000)

now, this is what i don't want:

i don't want racism,
sexism,
homophobia,
date rape,
serial killers,
cia dope dealers,
television evangelists,
and late night faith healers,
telemarketers,
politician fat cats,
cigarette companies,
lab rats,
traffic jams,
kids with guns,
parents with guns,
neighbors with guns,
cops
with guns,
coloured folks in cages,
minimum wages —
*when are we going to have a maximum wage?* —
road rage,
anger,
danger,
frustration,
loneliness,
depression,
futility,

slackers who support liberal causes yet can't be bothered to vote
and complain from their couches as our rights are taken away,

*most people don't want to know the truth. they just want to be happy.*

multinational corporations profiting from poisoning the
environment, raping human self-esteem, and co-opting culture,

mass media vultures spoon-feeding damage control as infotainment
*shiny tokens in a crow's face*
*as another poor man*
*faces another arraignment,*

i am tired of seeing a woman's precious body dismembered and
used to sell products: "look, breasts, buy this car! look, breasts, buy
this dvd!"

"is that your final answer?"
no, regis philbin!! as a matter of fact, i am just getting started!

now, this is what i do want:

i want happiness through art and expression, through interaction
with like-minded individuals who DO things rather than just TALK
about doing things, through risking embarrassment and rejection
and reaching out for that connection that makes life worth living.

i want good food free of poisons.

i want to walk into a market and buy my rice milk and veggies with
a poem instead of money.

i want everyone to know that i stole that last line from Allen
Ginsburg.

i want people to stop falling in love with songs on the radio and go
out and FALL IN LOVE for real and write their own love songs.

i want every vote cast in this country to actually be counted!

i want the president to be voted off the island, and i want aretha
franklin installed as president: "congress better R-E-S-P-E-C-T!
don't make me whip out my V-E-T-O!"

i want to pick up the phone and call mumia abu jamal and be like, "yo mumia, let's go pick up leonard peltier and go see that new jackie chan movie. And this time, you're paying."

i want my father to call me on the telephone and say, "hey son, i just wanted to say that i love you."

i want that last line to not make me cry anymore.

i want a tank full of gas and a sunny day and 1000 miles of open road with not a single traffic cop, cross street, or stop sign.

i want *calvin and hobbes* to come back... now!

i want a kick ass girlfriend who cries with me during that scene in *toy story 2* where sarah mclachlan is singing as the little girl takes her little cowgirl doll for a ride and the doll is so happy because she thinks they are finally going to play again, but no, she gets taken to the dump, and we both know how that feels, man!

i want a feast... i want a bean feast! cream buns and donuts and fruit cake with no nuts so good you could go nuts... daddy, i want an oompa-loompa now! *

i want love and passion not packaged as fashion, but as truth.

i want you, i want me, and i want no space between.

i want more than three minutes to finish this poem because there's a whole lot more that i want, that i don't want, that i need, and i want to tell you all about it..

* *lyrics from* i want it now *from* willy wonka and the chocolate factory

## **krakatoa** (2002)

my father was a skilled bbq technician
and every central californian summer
he would lay his magic hands on meat
and conduct grand operas
of seared flesh and glowing charcoal briquettes
lifting galloping symphonies of flame
to do his bidding

his backyard orchestra pit was nicknamed *krakatoa*
a mammoth bbq not store-bought
but hand-built
brick by concrete brick
until it loomed over us
a visual horrorshow bereft of aesthetics
but efficient beyond reproach

it was our fiery altar
to the gods of summer
and we worshipped weekly

when i was in high school
we were a few streets removed
from poor white trash
and couldn't afford grade a choice #1
so when my father bought meat
he had to pound it into submission
and i'm not talking with one of those
namby-pamby chrome-plated tenderizer mallets
from the kitchen section at *sears*, oh no,
my dad used a ball-peen hammer
from the garage

and he would knock the resistance
right outta that rump roast

cursing his day's frustrations away with every blow
attacking that t-bone till toughness fled shrieking
transforming cheap cuts of cow
into beef-flavoured butter
that melted at the gentle kiss of a fork

and while we stoked the coals
from the safety of shredded lawn chairs —
prodding porterhouses
charring chuck roasts
brushing and buttering and bbqing briskets and rib eyes —
we sat beside each other
and didn't say a word
just stared deep into the flames of *krakatoa*

him drinking a silver bullet of coors
me knocking back my brown bottle of ibc root beer
elvis on the a.m. radio

and it didn't matter
that i got crappy grades and cut class and
stole books from the mall and
played my depressing goth music too loud too late
and was probably on drugs
and probably gay
and probably a democrat
and probably going to amount to nothing
but a burden on my parents

and it didn't matter
that my dad and i didn't really speak anymore
that he understood me no better than i understood him
that he probably hated me as much as i hated him
that we were quickly becoming strangers
in our own home
more disgruntled housemates
who tolerated each other
than family

than father and son
than flesh...

okay, yeah, maybe all that stuff did matter
but in those moments at the grill
we could at least pretend
all that mattered
was making sure the steak had enough
secret recipe bbq sauce
so it wouldn't dry out

spreading the coals
to distribute the heat evenly
so no one got burned

just me and my dad
in the backyard
while my mother and sister
set the table inside
and never
ever
disturbed us

*no one will meet you the next time you fly into an airport.*

# the home front (1999)

to die brilliantly
was always the goal,
to tear at our schoolclothes
upon impact
of a well-aimed dirtclod
and tumble screaming and gurgling
from freshly erected mountains
of dark, moist earth
in a tangle
of scuffed Keds
and bowl cut hair,
to crumble
in a heap
with a weak "medic..."
spilling from our lips,
to heave a trembling sigh
and die
with our eyes half open
and our hands clutching
an invisible smoking carbine.

we were a motley crew of redneck kids
battling hordes of The Enemy
in the shadow of skeleton houses
at the outskirts of town,
crawling on our bellies
in the water pipe trenches
of soon-to-be strip malls and
convenience stores and
rows upon rows of cloned tract houses.

every saturday we met
while our parents watched family shows
on the teevee,

met in the field
cleared of trees and paved
with streets named *oak* and *birch*,
met by the scuffed yellow tractors and
earth movers and
dumptrucks
(tanks & jeeps & troop transports)
left by workmen over the weekend.

we
peppered our speech
with grizzled epithets
worthy
of combat
and bristling with battle-hardened authenticity:

*stop crying and fight like a man!*

*get off your ass and fight like a man!*

*stop crying before i give you a reason to cry! be a man!*

i remember
the last time
we played war.

john p.
crouched behind
a thick tangle of tumbleweeds
and hefted a fist-sized clod
embedded with concrete and weeds —
i heard it sizzle
as it missed my ear
by inches —
and nailed bo
right
between
the eyes.

bo,
who was always the point man
leading us into the thickest of battles,
who always died the most magnificent deaths,
who spewed paint-stripping obscenities
strange and venomous and wondrous to our ears,
whose body arced like a dying gull
through the air to collapse with a huff
onto the trampled earth
clutching severed limbs
and sucking chest wounds
and convulsing
with the most convincing
of death throes.

bo just stood there,
stunned
by the chunk of rock
embedded in his forehead,
and let a slender thread of red
carve a trail
through the dirt
of his nose.

we tensed,
waiting for the inevitable torrent
of curses that would become catchphrases
in the battles to come.

we watched
one bulbous drop
of real live blood
dangle from the curve
of his nostril
and splash on the laces
of his dirty white tennies.

*pain confirms existence.*

he glared at john p.,
then gary,
then mookie,
then me,
then tore the concrete from his head
and threw it with all his might
into the ground.

he mounted his bmx bike
and peddled
away.

*i'll give you a reason to cry*

the next saturday
it was just me and
gary's kid sister grace
swinging our legs
from the attic
of our favorite skeleton house
and talking in hushed tones
about the end
of summer.

*may 11, 1967*
*this was the day i was born. eleven days later, langston hughes died.*

# the sweet mysteries of hot peach cobbler (1999)

1.
12 years old
turning tricks in okie truckstops
my grandma
1938

she'd do anything
to get out of that dusty oklahoma town
        anything
to fade into the western sunset
to pick peaches penny a pound
in the Golden State
        in Lamont
        in Arvin
        in Wasco
        in Shafter

she'd lie
tell them she was 16
she'd lie
tell them she loved them
lie
on her back
in the dirty rags and boxes
of their pickup trucks

this pale slip of a blue-eyed farm girl

easy money
from a lonely man
600 miles from his home.
his wife.
his 12-year-old daughter.

*pearl harbor. normandy. iwo jima. guadalcanal. love.*

and their hot breath stank
of bathtub gin
and hand-rolled cigarettes

and their rough stubble
tore
at her skin
like a father's belt
and she held them all
tightly
and dreamed of palm trees
and fields and fields
of peach trees
ripe for the plucking.

2.
i watch my grandmother's hands
blurred by constant motion
and the gravity of age.

she slips the just sharpened knife
into the soft flesh
of her backyard peaches
and guides
the edge
along the unseen stone,
cracks open the virgin fruit
with a soft, wet ripping of ripe flesh
then peels the thin skin
with flicks of her thumb
against the blade.

she does this for an hour,
her hands pink and sticky with juice,
while i stir cinnamon and nutmeg
into boiling sugar syrup
and roll flour and salt and ice water
into dough.

*pedestals rob people of their humanity.*

later
we spoon the warm golden crisp
and golden bulbs of sweetness
into bowls
of cold milk —
pure childhood —
and she nods her head
as i smile the same grateful grandkid smile
i've had for years.

i do most of the work
when my grandmother makes
peach cobbler these days,
but she insists
on cutting her own peaches.

*pets feel uncomfortable around you.*

## **redneck** (2007)

i don't want to wear
*white* anymore
give me that redneck
my great grandad wore

while earning a quarter an hour
working central californian cotton fields
twenty cents an hour for potatoes
two and half cents
for a box of peaches
collected
in the scalding sun
so his barefoot family of 12
wouldn't starve

give me those rednecks
packed in the back of rickety model t's
and mule-drawn carts
with every possession
a cacophony of hungry children
aunties, memaws, cousins
everyone who could stand on the runners and
hang from the rumbleseat
by the calloused tips of their fingers
as they crawled down the back
of the mother road, route 66

you see
*white* doesn't remember
the acres of rich, black farmland laid waste
by shifting sands
evicting generations
and erasing histories
in the space of a season

*white* knows nothing of
border crossings in the silence of starlight
halted by los angeles police officers with shotguns
guarding every road, every bridge, every river
leading into the Golden State

"okie go home," they shouted,
"go back where you came from!"
"we already got ten men for every field job, now go home, okie,
and take your filthy, lice-ridden litter with you!"

newspapers warned of
*migrant hordes invading kern county*
and they weren't coming from mexico
they snuck over the arizona border
from shamrock, texas,
and godebowl, oklahoma

my family
my *white* family

while signs on every store
announced the owners would sooner
serve dogs than okies

you didn't just say that word
you spat it
then ground it into the dust
with the toe of your boot

redneck
recognizes the blood running through my veins
pumped from the hearts of the native american woman
and german fur trapper who began my family in america
blood
worked into the soil surrounding
california bergs like bakersfield and arvin and lamont

blood
that pulsed through hard-working families
forced to live in dirt-floored tent cities
and squatter camps that ringed towns like weedpatches

redneck
remembers *white* schoolchildren
being taught
that okies
were filth
okies
were scum
okies
were not *white*
they were animals that bred like vermin
and over-ran your cities
and infected your children
and drove workmen's wages
into the dirt through which they crawled

and yes
we were eventually allowed
the privilege of our *white* skin
through hard work and persistence
we were accepted
into a society
that even today
deprives people of colour
the right to live among equals

but *white* doesn't recognize
the shared struggle to belong
*okie* and *nigger* are two sides of the same filthy coin
that is the need of a privileged society
to find an *other* to blame for its ills
and push to its edge
and crush under the boot of prejudice

*pretend you're happy so no one gets uncomfortable.*

i have no pride in being *white*

that phrase assumes silver spoons
in the sepia-toned mouths
of the okies and rednecks whose sacrifice
allows me the freedom to be a poet
who writes about their struggles
rather than engages in them

yes, i benefit from white privilege every day
but do not forget
my neck —
as much as i've tried
to wash it clean —
is red

# poetry widow (1998)

to hell with poetry!
*she said,*
*the smoking gun of her finger in my face.*
to hell with poetry!
you don't write poetry for me anymore
you write excuses.
*oh, i've hurt your feelings again, here's a poem.*
*oh, i've disrespected your body again, here's a poem.*

to hell with poetry!

you're not a poet,
you're a snake-oil salesman.
you don't have relationships,
you have anecdotes.
i'm not your girlfriend,
i'm your material.
you take every sweet emotion we've shared
every intimate joy
every secret
and you twist them into laughter
at your stupid poetry slams.
that's not poetry,
that's grand theft.
you rob our relationship of meaning
in front of audiences
who cheer you on.

i used to love your poetry.
i was so flattered
the first time
you wrote a poem about me.
it was so sweet,
all that talk...

*curves in her hips and a smile on her lips
and a little round belly just like a real woman should*

but now i see right through you.

to hell with poetry!

you don't write poetry,
you write foreplay.
you write propaganda.
you prostitute your abilities
on self-centered conquests.
i'm not your muse —
your hunger for acceptance
your fragile self-esteem —
that's your muse.

to hell with poetry!

as a matter of fact, to hell with bukowski!
and to hell with ginsberg, too!
to hell with ferlinghetti and keruoac!
to hell with snyder and burroughs and rexroth.
to hell with sibilance and consonance
and assonance and alliteration!
to hell with free verse and sestinas
and quatranes and limericks and haiku!
to hell with iambic pentameter!
to hell with moon, spoon, june!
to hell with soulmate, partner, friend!
nothing is holy!
nothing is holy!
nothing is holy!
nothing... in your poetry... is holy...

to hell with poetry!

*romantic comedies are the opiate of the masses.*

i don't need your poetry, boy,
i need a man!
a man who doesn't hide
behind his *barnes & noble* journal
and his word processor.
i need a man.
you gonna be that man?
you gonna be my man?
or is momma gonna have to go shopping?

you want to create poetry for me?

fine.

put down your pen
and love me a poem.
respect me a poem.

listen:
i need you
to stop trying to find
the right words
and just

be

Poetry.

*ronald mcdonald is more recognized than jesus.*

## **passersby** (2003)

i am the one on the bus you shoulder past every morning on your way to work, the one with your favourite book in his backpack.

i am the one walking in the rain as you drive past and think to yourself how glad you are to be in a car instead of outside in the rain.

i am the waitress with the sniffly nose you didn't tip because you thought i took too long getting the lemon for your herb tea even though i apologized and didn't charge you for the tea because i thought you were cute.

i am the voice of the telemarketer who called at dinner, the one you hung up on in mid-sentence, the one who had more things in common with you than anyone you will ever meet, the one you'll never meet again for as long as you live.

i am the temp who closes her eyes and breathes the scent of your hair conditioner as you pass her in the hallway at work.

i am the 76-year-old woman who drove so on the freeway that you cursed her and honked at her and drove angrily past her, the one you would've fallen madly and deeply in love with had you only met her at 17 when she was a dancer and a poet.

i am the small woman with pale blue eyes who purchased an orange juice and a bagel every weekday morning at your cafe on her way to work for a year who got another job and moved away one day, the one you called *the oj girl,* the one you saw again years later while walking through a crowded airport in lexington, kentucky, but didn't recognize, the one who saw you and thought, "oh, *the bagel guy.*"

i am the man who lived in the apartment next to yours for years, the one who slept with his head inches from your pillow separated by a hand's breadth of drywall, wood, and space, the one you never met because he worked the graveyard shift, the one whose newspaper you borrowed every morning, read over breakfast, then carefully placed back in the plastic sack and returned to his front door as you left for work, the one with the cd collection nearly identical to your own.

i am your third grade sweetheart gazing out a bus window at an airplane passing thousands of feet overhead, the one who wonders whatever became of that little boy who would chase her around the jungle gym, the one who sighs deeply and turns back to her magazine as you gaze out the window of an airplane at the white roof of a bus stuck in traffic thousands of feet below and wonder how long it's been since you had a belly so swollen with laughter you could barely breathe.

i am the cable guy, the pizza guy, your mom's next door neighbor, the landlord, the counter girl, the mechanic, the cop, the paperboy, the exotic dancer at the all-nude strip club, everyone you've ever stood behind in lines, cut off in traffic, spoken with over the phone, dated, loved and lost, sat next to in a movie theatre, walked past on the sidewalk, taken a piss next to in subway bathrooms, purchased lattes from, whose lawns you mowed when you were a kid, who filled your tank, who rang you up, who changed your tire, who gave you a flier while walking past a bar a club a coffeehouse.

we pass within inches of you every single day.

we have so many stories to tell.

and you will never know any of them.

# the girl on the bus (1994)

she rides your bus every morning. sits in the very front, in the old people section.

she's pretty. knit gloves, corduroy jacket, sandals with thick socks. long light-red hair. young, maybe 19, 20, long and slender like a willow branch.

you don't know what color her eyes are, but she smiles your way almost every time she gets on the bus. it's a *yes-we-ride-the-same-bus-and-i-see-you-every-morning* smile, but it's friendly. she never shows her teeth when she smiles, but you bet they're straight. and white. you bet she smells like ivory soap and flowers, with a hint of patchouli oil.

she gets off two stops before you do, at the university, she and her backpack. she almost always pauses just before leaving, her hand curled around the silver rail along the wall, and flashes you a quick *i'll-see-you-on-the-bus-tomorrow* smile.

then, she's gone.

you work during the day. the bus drops you off a few blocks from the restaurant. you're a cook. 8-3, weekdays. you don't talk to the other cooks much. you just listen to their music — their banda, their salsa, their cumbias — and fry and flip and mix and stir and scoop and hand the waitresses their orders on greasy plates. during the winter the owner overcompensates for the cold outside and turns up the heat. in the dining room it's nice, but in the kitchen, with the grill and the fryers and the ovens, it's miserable. in no time, you're sticky with sweat, greasy balls of warm moisture crawling down your back.

the orders are all the same, variations on a theme. eggs, bacon or sausage, hotcakes or toast, maybe a hamburger steak or a ham steak or a new york steak. you don't have to think about it much. your hands know what to do. your eyes, too, taking in exactly what is needed from the scribbled orders ripped from the waitresses' pads.

your mind wanders.

*sex is the answer to all of your problems.*

you wonder what she does. probably lives at home, in the same bedroom she's lived in forever. maybe she lives in an apartment with roommates, two to a room to cut the rent in smaller pieces. maybe she lives on her own, with cats. tapestries and beaded things on the walls. a hand-me-down couch and love seat to match in the living room, a mattress on the floor in the bedroom. blue lights to replace the bright white ones. no television, but a nice birthday present stereo. maybe she buys all her cds used.

does she work? maybe she's a counter girl at some shop. maybe she works at a clothing store. not an antiseptic mall store, but a funky clothing store downtown. maybe she works at the s.p.c.a., caring for animals, or at an old-folks home. maybe...

"...cheese on their eggs..."

marti's talking. she's 7-3 today, 3 tables in section 2 and 4 in 3. she's holding a plate at you, her arm sticking through the window between the kitchen and the dining room. you ask what kind of cheese, she says cheddar, and you grab a handful and sprinkle it on top of her 2-egg scramble.

"thanks." she smacks her gum and walks away.

you look at the clock on the wall. 10:30. an hour and a half before your fifteen minute break. an hour and a half before you can wash some of this grease from your hands and face, before you can put your head under cold running water and pat your buzz-cut clean again. cleaner, anyway.

you get an order for a breakfast sandwich, no yolk. it's for liz, 10-4, section 5, by the bathrooms on the side. crack the egg, slop the yolk back and forth in the two halves of shell and let the clear white ooze into the metal *mason jar ring* on the grill that fries it in shape. open-faced english muffin half and a slice of american cheese. egg on top with a spatula. ladle the thick gravy, lumpy with sausage, but not too much. slide the plate of food onto the stainless steel shelf in the window, under the red heat lamp, with the order slip sticking from under the plate like a tongue. order up.

later, 6:15, and you're walking the eight blocks downtown to the university, the collar of your blue workshirt still wet from head-soaking. you're running a little late for your 6:30 class. child development, a general education class. you like to get there a bit early to finish the reading you're usually behind on. plus, it allows you to sit in the very back, away from everyone. you're sure the sponge bath in the deep sink at work does little to hide the fry cook smell.

   it's dark outside, and cold, by the time class ends. you walk to the bus stop two blocks away. get onto the bus. go home.

 and you read. do homework. watch teevee. shower. go to sleep. in your single bed, wedged up against a wall under the window, you look up through the venetian blinds at the trees. at the trees. at the moon. at the stars.

   the next morning is full of rain and cold. by the time the bus comes to your stop, you are soaked to the skin, shoes bleeding cold water and mud. you slosh over to your usual seat, in the middle, next to a window, and pull out a book from your dripping backback.

   two stops later — at her bustop — only the two high school kids get on.

## sorrow - part two (2003)

edmund loved sad songs.

he collected them like some people collect stamps. he had japanese pop tunes that made his heart ache, mississippi blues riffs that caused tears to burst from his eyes, pakistani folks songs he could not begin to understand that made him bury his face in his pillow at night just thinking of them.

and he wondered how the sound of a bow drawn across the strings of a violin could conjure within him the forlorn thoughts of lost loves and dashed hopes, how breath blown over an oboe's reeds could bring him to his knees and weep.

and he wondered what those sounds had in common with the distant longing sound of train whistles, the mournful wail of wolves howling, the wind in the tops of willow trees.

edmund felt if he could isolate the roots in all of these sad sounds, he might be able to arrange the notes into one chord, the playing of which would connect all the sad songs ever sung and all the sad sounds ever heard and bring forth an unstoppable human tide of glorious and well-earned tears.

and one day, after much labor, he found it.

and he organized a performance in a grand hall, and he invited members of the world press to come and encouraged them to broadcast the event simultaneously to all corners of the globe.

and on the night of the performance, edmund stood in front of his keyboard in a somber grey tuxedo and tails and a tall smoky stovepipe hat, and he cleared his throat, and he said very softly into the microphone, "and now, ladies and gentlemen of the world, i give you my gift... *the chord of ultimate sadness.*"

and the whole wide world held its breath.

and edmund brought his grey-gloved hand down softly on the keys.

and there issued forth from speakers all around the planet — from every radio station, from every television station, from every web browser — pure and beautiful and complete... silence.

and fat laughing buddhas with huge flapping earlobes danced waltzes down the cheeks of the whole wide world.

and edmund closed his eyes, lowered his head, and smiled.

*smile... you're a slave... go buy a pepsi.*

## not drowning, but waving (2006)

when zara cries
she withdraws into herself
pulls fist-sized knees to her chest
and wraps slender arms tight
around them
buries her face
red
in the tiny hollow she creates
with her whole body
using everything she has
to protect herself
from further hurt

and i am so moved
by the sight of her so small

i want to hold every bit of her
whisper tears away
tell her everything will be okay
even when we both know it won't be
if i can only hold her tight enough
warm enough long enough
with all of me enough
until everything is okay

i love her so much
i can stop trains
with my upturned palms

when we swam in galveston
in a warm ocean of inside jokes and smiles
wrist-strapped to boogie boards on whitecaps
i was always aware of the distance
between us

*february 20, 1985*
*zara was born on this date.*

aware of her narrow shoulders
pressed against those waves
the rip tide tugging at my ankles
so eagerly sucking her from my grasp

and i called to her
beckoning her closer
held her hand as the biggest waves broke
over our heads and battered us
always ready to leap through the current
grab her ankle
save her
from washing out to sea

once or twice
i found myself alone in the ocean to my neck
tossed
eyes blurred with salt and sand and sunscreen
grasping in vain for my lover's fingertips
only to look behind me
and see her seaweedy head
pop up near the shore
having just caught the perfect wave
and smiling

*strive to be different just like everybody else.*

## **tigerlily** (2004)

a key to understanding her is understanding tigerlily.

she introduced me to tigerlily about two weeks after we met. tigerlily is what she calls her period, and there's a magical lilt to her voice when she speaks of it, and a gravity.

all the girls at the treatment center where she'd spent six months named their periods. it was a ritual of healing and rebirth, a sacred ceremony marking the time when her tiny body had healed enough to bleed again, a celebration that the 75 pounds of flesh wrapping her thin bones had blossomed to 85 or 90 pounds, just enough to flick hidden switches in her body and reawaken the dormant womanhood held captive by hunger.

when she bled again for the first time, she wept ferociously, reclaiming her body and reconnecting to every curve and hollow, refusing for good the fight of finger and throat that burned her tongue with acid and etched the enamel from her smile and distanced her soul from her flesh.

the other night, we walked to the 24-hour restaurant near campus holding hands and smiling. as we talked and absent-mindedly rubbed bare legs together under the table like grasshoppers, she picked bits of my blueberry pancake and plopped them into her mouth, little bites, and i realized it was the first time i had ever seen her eat.

she still struggles. she's a vegetarian who skips lunches too often. she smokes too much. she still drinks diet coke. her 5'1" frame is all gossamer and willow branches, but there's a determination in her gaze that radiates to every limb, a solemn promise she made to herself to never again drive tigerlily away.

# someone (2003, 2007)

someone quicker to laugh than rage. someone who does things rather than sit on the couch talking about doing things. someone who makes things. someone who makes things happen. someone who watches the news and gets angry and wants to do something about it. someone who can appreciate a long, deep breath full of summertime after being pelted by swollen raindrops the size of baby fists. someone who can sit on a couch under a blanket and read with me while nick drake is playing on the stereo, sipping chamomile tea with lemon and honey and touching hips. someone who will look me in the eye and tell me i am wrong, but who doesn't always have to be right. someone who can have an effortless conversation lasting hours, but who isn't afraid of silence. someone who enjoys debating movies and politics and what happens after you die. someone who enjoys lazy bike rides across long bridges and back alleys. someone who would rather see local theatre than watch teevee, but who also appreciates that *the office* and *lost* make teevee almost worth watching every once in a while sometimes maybe a little kinda. someone who isn't afraid to dance even though they secretly know they look silly when they dance, but it's okay since everyone looks silly when they dance. someone who can't pass a jell-o butt puppy without patting its wee scruffy head. someone who has favourite words and goes out of their way to use them regularly. by the way, my favourite words are: *succotash, scallywag, shindig,* and *brouhaha.* someone who yearns for travel and adventure, but who also appreciates the lure of tire swings on old oak trees. someone with their act together... most of the time. someone who doesn't take themselves so seriously that they can't laugh at themselves. someone who will stick up for what they believe in, especially if i don't believe in it. someone who can kick my butt at scrabble, balderdash and cranium. someone who can actually spell *brouhaha.* someone who can appreciate the joy of mix tapes. someone who spoons. someone who kicks ass. someone who has lofty goals they can actually taste. someone who has gotten their heart torn apart and has learned to sew it back together all by themselves. someone who appreciates hand-made birthday cards and homemade cakes that are kinda lopsided but honest.

*(pause)*

b-r-o-u-h-a-h-a.

# real live über grrl (1997)

let me tell you about my girl.

she is... beautiful. she's got curves in her hips and a smile on her lips and a little round belly just like a real woman should. when she smiles, she glows, like ten thousand fireflies caught in a woman-shaped bottle, and when she smiles at me, oh... she just melts me like an ice cube in a frying pan.

sometimes she's quiet and shy and lowers her head when she's embarrassed. sometimes she's in my face with an idea that burns in her mind and flickers in her eyes. and sometimes she raises her hands in the air and shakes them when she's frustrated and growls at the messed up way the world is. and sometimes she just puts her head on my shoulder and pats my hairy belly and tells me she likes me a whole lot.

we can spend a 9-hour roadtrip just talking and talking about this and that and the other thing and — boom — suddenly, we're there. and we can just sit at opposite ends of her bed, each with a book, and not say a single word for hours except with our toes under the covers.

the woman in my life has hairy legs. this may not mean a lot to you, but to her it's a statement. it's a manifesto. she loves being a woman, everything about being a woman: the blood, the softness, the struggles, the sisterhood, and the space she has deep inside that she allows to be filled only in the way she chooses. the woman in my life loves her armpits. the smell of them, the taste of them, the feel of them, the wild bush of unkempt armpit hair so thick you could grow tomatoes in them, and you know what? i feel the same way about them.

this is a woman in complete control of her womanhood, and if your fragile masculinity can't handle it, boy, that's your problem.

*taboos are society's way of controlling you.*

the woman in my life is a complete person. she has no desire to be a square peg for some dumb boy to force into his round hole, nor does she want to be used as a bridge or an umbrella or a scented handkerchief.

sometimes she lets me sleep on the good pillow, next to the wall, just how i like it. sometimes she tells me to have a nice night and walks herself to her door. and sometimes she taps on my window and asks very politely through my screen if i know any warm places she can sleep.

i've wanted to write a poem about her since the day i met her, but i won't. depriving the world of one more crappy love poem will probably do my karma some good.

*technology brings people closer, like cattle.*

## crushworthy (1999)

i want someone
to have a crush on me
    for a change

to notice
when i don't come to class
and wonder if i'm okay

to get nervous
when i enter the cafe,
to fumble
with her papers
and books,
to pick at her clothing
and check
her reflection
in salt shakers and napkin holders

to catch her breath
when she sees me from across campus,
tug on her best friend's collar
and point with her eyes
and whisper loudly,
"there he is...
big poppa e!"

to run around the block
as quickly
— and nonchalantly —
as she can
just to walk past me
make eye contact
and smile

*that pain you are ignoring is probably cancer.*

to look into my big brown eyes
*such long lashes!*
from across the room
and think, "yesss..."
to look at my full kissing lips
and think, "oh yesss..."
to hear my voice
and imagine
how her name
would sound
if i said it
if i whispered it
if i...

*oh yesss...*

i want someone
to make up nicknames for me
to talk about me in code
"i saw *Backpack Boy* today
in the library
in the romantic lit. section!
i saw *Steel-Toed Boots Boy*
talking to some girl
*some girl!*
in the bookstore today!"

i want someone
to go straight home every night
and check her answering machine
just in case
just in case
and check the phone cord
and check the battery
and check the tape
and make sure the damn blinking light
isn't burned out
just in case i called

*that person you have a crush on is afraid of you.*

i want someone to say,
"you're wrong about him
because you don't know him
the way i know him!"

because she can just    tell
i'm a good person
must be
a good person
gotta be
a good person
because i write poetry about my grandma and my cats
and because she likes me so much
for some reason
some unexplainable psychic supernatural reaction
to me

me

i want someone
to mark her calendar
*he talked to me today*

to wonder
what i would smell like
after a long warm sleep
under a down comforter

to close her eyes
and picture
what our kids would look like

to write silly wretched wonderful
poetry
about me
for a change

## there's a hole in my heart in the shape of her smile that will never be filled (2000)

*for jen*


i will never forget
the last sentence
of the article in the newspaper
the next day:

*the terrible crash pancaked the tiny honda civic*

it rattled our minds
as we ran our fingers
across the gouges
in the pavement,
our eyes squinting
through a thousand glaring pinpricks
from windshield fragments,
searching
for lucky pennies
scattered
hundreds of them
from her broken penny jar.

*the terrible crash pancaked the tiny honda civic*

that sentence robbed us of closure.

we weren't allowed to marvel
at the mortician's handiwork.
*she looks like she's asleep.*
we couldn't cup
her lifeless hand —

powdered
and coloured
with an artist's touch —
and confirm
that it was true
that it actually really
had happened.

no, the terrible crash pancaked the tiny honda civic, and they
wouldn't even run photos because it's a family newpaper and you
can't run photos like that in a family newspaper.

we had to just
agree
nod our heads in unison
and agree that she was gone
and would never be back

this precious flower
plucked
in mid-blossom.

and we held each other
and remembered her
as we had last seen her
pink and alive and smiling
that big thumbs up smile

and we were warmed by the knowledge
that if anyone could've changed the world
she could've.
she would've
had she only been given the chance.

but now...

we'll always feel like she's out there
somewhere

*the only true love is unrequited love. all else is compromise.*

always at the corner of our eyes
in the summer sea of spaghetti straps and backpacks
tan lines and smiles
she'll be there
and we'll catch our breath
turn
and see nothing.

i think about that last sentence every time i drive, it echoes in my
brain as i near the spot on the four-lane highway where she crossed
the median and died.

i picture the time of day: around 11 a.m.

the sun was out. the sky was blue. there was no rain.

she was driving alone. she was probably smoking.
she was listening to *james taylor's greatest hits;*
we know this because the tow crew
pried that cd from what was left of her stereo.

and i grip my wheel white-knuckled
as i near the spot.

and i can't help counting down
the time she had left.
(and she didn't even know it was coming.)

it was a bright sunny day and she was singing...

*i've seen fire and i've seen rain*
20 seconds

*i've seen sunny days that i thought would have no end*
10 seconds

*i've seen lonely times when i could not find a friend*
5 seconds

*but i always thought i'd see you baby one more time again...\**

and just like that we are past it
and the scars in the pavement are left behind.

and just like that we are past it
and the white cross we left in the grass
on the embankment is left behind.

and just like that we are past it
and the lucky pennies
and the photos
and the little good luck tokens
and the letters
and the constellations of shattered windshield
are left behind.

just like that    she
was left behind.

the headline should not have read
*chico state university student killed in car crash.*

no, the headline should've shouted in capitol letters
across the front page:

*JENNIFER LYNN O'HARE KICKED SO MUCH ASS!*

she was a poetess, a priestess, a goddess, a feminist, a fighter,
a lover, a laugher, a teller of truths, a spinner of midnight balcony
tales shrouded in heineken and camels...

she could break down brian johnson's male chauvinest arguments
with the precision of a surgeon, hurling words like *patriarchal* and
*misogyny* and *hegemony* in a rapid fire distillation of everything
she had learned in women's studies classes. we almost felt sorry for
brian as she leaned towards him on the edge of her stool pointing
with the glowing cherry of a lit cigarette...

*the world is run by weak, insecure men who need spankings.*

she was a god-awful drummer but a very enthusiastic drummer, a deep and passionate kisser, a liver of life, a lover of all things, not the best of students but the best of teachers, a mentor, a sister, a daughter, a confidant, a friend... my friend.

these words should have been displayed on the pages
of every newspaper in the world.

but they were

most people in this world probably didn't even realize their loss.

and i feel sorriest of all for those people — you people—
those of you who never had the chance to meet her.

she was *that* cool.

the last sentence
in this poem
is how i will remember
jennifer lynn o'hare:

this world is a better place for having jen in it,
even if it was for only 20 years.

*lyrics from james taylor's* fire and rain

*they'll never allow you to be cool.*

*think globally. act nonchalantly.*

*time flies when you're not paying attention.*

*toilets are the great equalizers.*

*true love. greeting cards. romantic comedies. big foot.*

*visualize anarchy.*

*voting is for fools. apathy creates true change.*

*wallow in your weakness.*

*we are drowning in a sea of stimuli.*

*we are slaves to cats.*

*we can see right through you.*

*we hate most in others what we hate in ourselves.*

*what do you think you're doing?*

*what would they think about your dirty little secret? want to find out?*

*what you think is love is actually fear of being alone.*

*when you die the universe goes with you.*

*wristwatches are shackles.*

*you are a goddess.*

*you are in the control group.*

*you are more beautiful than you could ever imagine.*

*you are not innocent.*

*you are on display.*

*you are patient zero.*

*your 12-year-old self would be so disappointed to meet you now.*

**PROPERS** speech competition kids have been covering work from poetry slammers for several years, and when school's in session, i get several requests from high school and college kids each week asking for permission to perform my stuff at regional and national speech competitions. i wrote this piece at the request of a high school kid from west texas with red dreadlocks at a big conference at west texas a&m during my spring 2004 tour. she asked me to write a poem for her, and 20 minutes later, i performed this piece in front of 300+ kids. i ended up performing it for the sixth season of hbo's *def poetry* in 2006, and i dedicated it to *the girl from west texas with red dreadlocks*. **THE WISDOM OF SCARS** the time between graduation and so-called real life can be such a wonderfully painful and bewildering time for both the person going through it and their parents. it's a constant wrestling match between one's own sense of self and the idea their parents had in mind when conceiving the baby who would become this individual beyond their complete control. it's a struggle, and it tests and defines the relationship between parent and child from that time on, i think. i wrote this poem for two precious people going through that time, one just graduated from high school and the other having just finished college and moving into the scary real world: sisters aimy and zara. i love them both very much, and i hope their scars never obscure their intense beauty. **MISSION STATEMENT** a college student i met while performing at texas a&m university in fall 2004 emailed me and asked me who i was, meaning, like, who i was in a deep sort of meaningful way. i thought about it for a bit, then i wrote this and emailed it to her. it pretty much captures the way i feel about what i do. painfully beautiful. achingly lovely. **¡THE WUSSY BOY MANIFESTO!** if any poem threatens to be my *stairway to heaven*, it's this one. the words to this piece will probably be etched into my tombstone. it started as scribbles in the margin of the notebook i used for a communications class in february of '99. i had come up with the concept of using *wussy* as an empowering term a couple of years before i wrote the poem, but it didn't come together until the notes were compiled in this communications class. it was pretty effortless and natural. now it's become something much bigger than i ever expected. i had signature poems before this one, but now everything i've ever done will be eclipsed by it. i suppose i can handle that. feel free to change the specific wussies i mention to keep the piece current. **FALLING IN LIKE** i just wrote this poem in the middle of putting this book together, and i liked it so much that i added it and had to switch around all the page numbers and the table of contents and all that. i love the idea of liking someone so much you just lose all your cool, leaving you feeling completely innocent and awed by the intensity of it all. this was written as a collaboration with zara, my best friend in the whole world. she came up with the ideas about quizzing each other with dueling dictionaries, trading the jelly sandwich, the green crayon, the chicken pox, and making the valentine's day card with sparkles and glue, then i rewrote them and added my stuff. i feel this way about zara all the time. we woulda been the best of friends had we known each other at 12. **ODE TO DWARF PLANET 134340** gotta represent the underdog, even if it's a heavenly body at the far reaches of our solar system. pluto knows nothing of our obsessive need to define it, and i suppose it wouldn't care even if it did. pluto is what it is, and that never changes, no matter what label you attach to it. a lot of my very favourite people are like pluto. i'm like pluto. maybe you're like pluto, too. this is not really a poem at all, just a list of applause lines, but it always seems to stir up emotion. you wouldn't think defending a planet would rouse such emotion, but people really feel it for some

*you need to document your life, or else you'll disappear.*

reason. **CLOSER TO THE HEART** the first 45 rpm records i ever got my hands on were loaned to me by david pletcher, my best friend in my freshman year of high school, and one of them was the single for rush's *tom sawyer* with *witch hunt* as the b-side. i can't honestly say listening to that 45 changed my life, but it sure did make me a huge fan of the band. they were, in fact, my very first god band, followed in rapid succession by pink floyd, led zeppelin, the police, u2, and foetus. i bought everything rush ever did, and i still have everything they did up to *exit... stage left.* after that, they started to suck, and i didn't have the heart to watch something so dear die such an unworthy and drawn-out death. their most recent stuff harkens back to their glory days, but it will never be the same as when i was 14 and miserable and alone. maybe the fact that i find myself miserable and alone more often than not lately is why i've returned to them for solace, endlessly listening to them on repeat on my ipod. **EMO LOVE SONG IN THE KEY OF 9-3/4** i was aware of the *harry potter* phenomenon going back to, like, 2001, when my poetry friend and then-roomie morris stegosaurus practically demanded that i read the books, but i resisted, seeing the crazed look of an addict in his eyes. like i needed another obsession. i ended up giving in during a tour across the u.s. in the summer of 2003, and i devoured each and every book. i've been a fan ever since. this song is just a simple little ode to adolescent yearning, the story of a teenaged boy crushing on his best friend and not knowing quite what to do about it. we've all been there. i crushed on everyone when i was 13 and lived and died at the merest sneezes in my direction. still do. **WALLFLOWER** every so often i skim through my online journal in the hopes of finding possible poems lying in wait. this one started as a few sentences describing this college house party my immature college roomies took me to once. i felt so stupid and clumsy being there, but ended up fascinated by the way all the girls moved. it was amazing. truth be told, i am actually not that bad of a dancer. this was put together over a few weeks in early 2002. **JESUS MOSHPIT** i wrote this on a budweiser napkin at a punk show in chico, ca, in the fall of '96. it was a first date with kimberly, the muse for way too many of my poems, and she was writing a story on a little punk band called *no use for a name* for the university newspaper. i felt so wimpy watching the moshpit full of shirtless punks in their prime, clashing into each other and impervious to the pain. it's nice to imagine what it would be like to be the biggest guy in the moshpit, so big that not even god would want to mess with you. ah, wussy boy fantasies. when i look back, this is probably the very first big poppa e poem, even though i wrote it a few years before the name came up. **NAPOLEON** i am really surprised to see this piece again, having dismissed it as a failure. i just never really got along with this piece, even though audiences tended to like it okay. it never really gelled with me, so i put it away and swore to never perform it again. then, about a year later, i happened upon it while looking for something to read at the san antonio slam, and it wasn't all that bad, so i made some quick edits, added some new lines, and voila! i got the highest score of the night! i did it again the next night at the austin slam, and i practically got a standing ovation. so weird... i had given up on this poem, but it wouldn't go away. **CHAIN RECORD STORE BLUES** i hate retail. i hate malls. i hate christmas. this piece has nothing to do with poetry and everything to do with lashing out at the very people who are causing you pain. in this case, the shallow capitalist dogs who fill malls the day before xmas. i wrote it while working at a record store called the wherehouse in chico, ca, around dec. of '97 or maybe '98. i can't remember. i stole so many cds from that job, which i don't recommend, because stealing is bad, and i totally got caught and fired for it. i was lucky they didn't call the po-po. **FLOSS** this is an oldie, written for a zine i once did back in the day, probably around '94. i hadn't even heard of poetry slamming at that point, but this piece ended up being the first one i performed at my very first slam at the taos poetry circus in '96. it was my first signature piece, and for a long time, yeah, I was the guy who does the floss poem. and yes, I am really that freaky about flossing. **OH! CANADIAN FEDEX LADY!** this pretty much actually happened the way it's implied. i was working the phones at apple computer and was completely taken with the cute voice of the canadian fedex lady who was helping me track an order, and i actually did leave my customer on hold long enough to get the basic idea of this piece in my journal so i could finish it later. we didn't really flirt — i was with zara at the time, and she woulda cutta fool — but what cracks me up is the idea of flirting with a cute voice... it's just so silly! plus i really like the stilted references to canada, as if the speaker really doesn't know all that much about canada at all except what he could find on wikipedia, yet he's still trying his best to impress this canadian crush. i ended up performing this piece for the annual apple computer employee talent show, and i was fired two days later because it was deemed unprofessional. whatevs. the video i made about the situation — *why i got fired from apple computer* — ended up getting a million hits on youtube and google video, and about a bzillion websites linked to it. it was really bizarre to be famous on the internet for about, oh, a week or so, at least until the next video of someone lighting his farts came along. **DISILLUSION CURRY** this actually, really happened. this girl really did exist, and she really did have a pepsi logo tattooed on her arm. i think i'll get a nike swoosh across my forehead. **THE DOUBLE GLASS DOORS OF YOUR HEART** this cat named andy buck was my teammate on the '02 austin poetry slam team, and he posted the beginnings of a poem on his online journal that said something about "if you had a full body tattoo of the globe, i would circumnavigate your tummy"... i don't know, some crap like that, and it cracked me up and made me roll my eyes, so i immediately posted this ode in my journal the next day as a means of ribbing him. i performed it at the next slam and got a really good response, so it's been in heavy rotation ever since. i suppose i could say it has a deeper meaning than is apparent, but no, it doesn't, it's just me messing around at andy's expense. **IMMORTALIZED IN CELLULOID** a really good way for me to get the hint that i am really depressed is by noticing how many movies i am seeing at any given time. the more movies and dvds, the more i am needing to escape whatever it is that i don't want to deal with. while I was in seattle in 2001, i was a movie-watching monster, renting dvds by the fistfuls and catching movies nearly every friday night, mostly all by myself. it's easy to want to escape into that world where everything works out, we all fall in love, everything is cool, and the drama we experience is only to make the happy ending more worthwhile. i first wrote this in '98 or so, then I dusted it off in seattle in spring of 2001 and cleaned it up a bit. **13 METAPHORS FOR WHY WE SHOULD'VE NEVER DATED** sometimes we are absurdly attracted to the very people who are worst for us, and yet we can't seem to help ourselves, can we? i suppose the inspiration for this was a girl named mandy who i met in albuqurque. cool chick in many ways, but absolutely wrong wrong wrong for me in so many more ways, which made her irresistible. what's up with that? and yes, i realize there aren't exactly 13 metaphors, but i think that makes it even funnier, so shut up. **DEATH WISH** this was a column i published in the chico state university student newspaper *the orion*, but i've read it a couple of times at slams to pretty good reaction, so i've included it here in case i ever want to read it again. i am terrifically afraid of death, and if i could choose to never die, i would make that choice in about a millisecond. i really need to get over that fear, but i have no idea how. if you have any ideas, let me know. **RECEIPT FOUND IN THE PARKING LOT OF THE SUPER WALMART** no, silly, i didn't really find this receipt in the parking lot of a super walmart. some people are so gullible. i just wanted to write a poem with nothing more than a list of items so that the whole story and the whole plot is merely suggested by the order of the items, and the audience has to fill in the rest. this was one of the very few poems i wrote while in seattle, probably around may of 2001. whenever i go to the supermarket, i try to figure out who the people in line are by looking at their groceries on the conveyor belt. my favourite part is the cat food at the end. **ROADTRIPPIN'** oh, the majesty of the road. i wrote an early version of this one while driving to the taos poetry circus in '96. and i mean while actually driving, like knee on the steering wheel, pen in one hand, journal in the other, driving down the highway at 95 mph. it's been rewritten several times since then, including an ill-advised version with me singing to the songs on the radio during the trip... ugh, I really don't need to be singing in any poem, believe me, and that version was immediately scrapped. **LEAVING LAS VEGAS** it was really reno, summer of '99, but *leaving reno* just didn't have the right ring to it. i really have to control my breathing on this one, otherwise the long tongue-twisty lines use up all my oxygen and break my rhythm. it's okay, this one, my attempt at doing a political poem, I guess. **POEM FOR A FRIEND** i was going to be in a poetry slam at a venue that was primarily black in early '99, and i tried to write a poem that would appeal specifically to that audience, or, at least, to what i thought that audience would like. my friend looked at the poem i was about to deliver, and he tore me a new ass for trying to pander to the audience. he told me to stop trying to impress people with how *down* i was and just deliver my truth, which is all any audience ever wants. i ended up doing *wussy boy,* which is about as true to me as i can get, and it went over great. lesson learned. this poem tries to illustrate that lesson. **OPEN LETTER** the members of the poetry slam community keep in contact with each other via the internet, including a yahoo groups list serve, and a straight white american male poet who shall go nameless posted a message in spring of 2004 stating how he felt discriminated against since he could never, ahem, *play the race card.* whatever, dude. how's about you just write some freakin' poetry and shut up about that crap? anyway, this was my response. i doubt he's ever seen it, but if he had, i can imagine he probably was like, "yeah! i hate people like that!" idiot. i have to admit this piece was based on something i found on the internet called a *white privilege checklist,* written by (i think) someone named peggy mcintosh. this is my version, and i may have stolen a line or two and ran with them. sorry, peggy, whoever you are. if you want to see her version, just google it. and yes, again, i know there aren't exactly 20 reasons listed, but i still think that's funny, so shut up. **PUSHING BUTTONS** this poet named kenny mostern in san francisco was slamming against me one night in '99 or '00, and he bet me a dollar that he could outscore me. i told him that not only could i outscore him, but I could write a piece off the top of my head right then and there and score a perfect 30. he stifled a laugh and bet me a dollar. when he scored a 29.6, which is pretty damned close to perfect, he was sure he had me beat. nope, sad to say, this poem scored a 30 it's first time out. it's such a shameless display of button pushing, and i often serve it up as a mocking example of how easy it is to write a crowd-pleasing slam piece. i suppose there is an art to being shamelessly crowd-pleasing, but I still feel guilty when I do this poem and get phat applause for it even though i truly believe in every word of it. **KRAKATOA** i wanted to write a poem about my dad that wasn't all negative and stuff, but it was hard. we've had our challenges, that's for sure. he still can cook a mean steak. what the man can do with a piece of filet mignon is fascinating. **THE HOME FRONT** this was a creative writing class poem circa late '99. i've rarely slammed it and when i have, it always gets crappy scores. whatevs. i like it, though, because of the images and the sort of oratorical patterns in it. it's fun to perform. **THE SWEET MYSTERIES OF HOT PEACH COBBLER** my grandma ott told me at gunpoint to stress to the world that this poem is not about her, not even in the slightest bit. yeah, she has blue eyes, but that's it. the rest is all made up. there, grandma, i told them. this poem came to me as i was falling asleep one night in late '99. i was going to blow it off and write it down in the morning, but huge chunks started disappearing as i faded, so i rolled over and wrote it down on a scrap of paper in the dark next to my bed. by the morning, i had completely forgotten it. had i not seen the paper several days later, it would've been another poem that got away. **REDNECK** i get really tired of poetry slammers who are white complaining about how they are not allowed to *pull the race card.* idiots. but i also get tired of people thinking that just because my skin is white that my family has never had to struggle with prejudice in this country. it's simply not true. ask the irish in new york city in the turn of the century. ask okies. ask gay people or women or anybody in a wheelchair. discrimination has no boundaries, it's just about ignorance and hate, and you can hate anybody for any reason, even when you have to invent that reason. **POETRY WIDOW** i often found that i would write these sappy little love poems for my college girlfriend kimberly every time i did something lame and hurtful. it was cheaper than flowers, you know? but, towards the end of our relationship, she would look at me suspiciously when i gave her a poem about her, as if she were waiting to hear my latest excuse for messing up. i performed this piece for the first time at the '98 finals for the san francisco poetry slam. everyone told me not to debut an untested piece at a finals slam that would pick the official slam team, but i did it anyway. i cried during it because kimberly was in the audience and had never heard it. she cried, too. after the piece, i waded through the crowd and hugged her as everyone cheered. i got the highest score of the night. it was just like a scene from *fame.* this piece is inspired by a poem by etheridge knight called *feeling f\*\*\*ed up.* it's sort of my version of it. it also riffs a bit on ginsberg's *howl* with the *nothing is holy* parts. check it out. you'll see what i mean. **PASSERSBY** this poem is so unfinished that i almost didn't include it. i really need to re-write it and tighten it up because it's nothing more than notes for a poem rather than a poem itself. one of these days i'll finish it. i like the idea of looking at passing traffic and realizing how many lives are held within each car, lives i'll never know. **THE GIRL ON THE BUS** another creative writing class endeavor, this one from late '94 when i first moved to chico, ca. i like this one a lot. even though it's verse, i think it's very poetic. there actually was a *girl on the bus* who was the inspiration for this poem, a very beautiful red-haired girl who caught my attention on the way to school on the bus. when the story was finished, i gave her a copy. i would see her every now and then, and i would always think, "say, it's *the girl on the bus.*" **SORROW, PART TWO** i have no idea where this one came from, but i do know that i was walking through a grassy field in athens, texas, near the house of my then-girlfriend's grandma when it came to me. by the time the walk was through, so was the poem, and after a few last-minute edits, it was done. i suppose silence is the saddest sound i can think of. **NOT DROWNING BUT WAVING** i wrote this about zara and a trip we took to the beach at corpus christi, texas. it's about that time in a relationship where you have to consider your options, when you think that you could break up any second, and you struggle with that, struggle between wanting to hold on with all your might and allowing your relationship to move naturally from one of lovers to one of friends. sometimes you have to let go and allow things to end if you really want it to last forever. hold on too tight, and it could kill it. the title is a riff off *not waving but drowning* by stevie smith. **TIGERLILY** i met a girl here in austin in fall of 2004, a fragile drama girl addicted to meth and anorexia who was trying very hard to leave both behind and failing. she was trouble, i knew it the moment i laid eyes on her, but that didn't stop us from spending time together for a few months. we had the same birthday... how could i resist? i wrote this about her just a few weeks after we'd met, and she cried. she said i was the only person who had ever gotten it right. in the end, she was way too dramatic, and we stopped hanging out, but this poem remains. i hope she's okay. **SOMEONE** this was actually written in response to the question *what are you looking for in a mate?* on one of those online personal ad websites. admitting this makes me feel really lame, like are you serious? you perform in front of audiences all over the country, and you can't find a freakin' date? well... yes... actually... i'm kinda shy. leave me alone. wanna hear a joke i invented? question: how many big poppa e's does it take to screw in a lightbulb? answer: zero, because he'd rather sit in the dark in his room all alone and cry. **REAL LIVE ÜBER GRRL** another in a series of kimberly poems written during our three-year relationship. this was one of the first, penned in '97 probably. i look at it now and see it for what it is, really, which is less a description of her and more of my idea of the perfect girlfriend. i liked kimberly a whole lot for quite some time, though, even though neither of us was all that perfect. **CRUSHWORTHY** jennifer lynn o'hare was the impetus for this poem, and i wrote it very shortly after meeting her for the first time at a slam in chico, ca, around spring of 1999. she was so cute, sitting there in the front row making all kinds of eye contact with me as i hosted the slam. when I presented this poem to her a few days later, she ran into her bedroom and came out with her journal to show me that she had written a poem exactly like it. we dated for six months after that. she was such a cool girl. really beautiful in every way. **THERE'S A HOLE IN MY HEART IN THE SHAPE OF HER SMILE THAT WILL NEVER BE FILLED** i can't believe it's already been eight years since jen died. once we started dating, she was always asking me, "when are you going to write another poem about me?" i would hem and haw and say something about poetry not being fast food you could just order up hot and fresh at the drive-thru, but I always told her that more poetry would come in its own sweet time. i never in a million years would've guessed that the next poem i would write about jen would be this one. i spent the months following jen's death in a fit of writer's block, not being able to write anything, but then, just a week before my national tour in summer of 2000, i finally was able to write this poem. and i was finally able to cry. **I GUESS THAT'S IT** it is 4:29 p.m. on july 4, 2007. as i type this on my ibook, i'm listening to a group named *i am robot and proud*, and zara is at my imac designing websites. it's raining very heavily outside, and the kitties are chilling with me on the futon chair. i have given my one-month notice at work, and i am about to start booking gigs for a long national tour. i just bought the coolest backpack ever on ebags.com, and i am so in love with it, i want to marry it and have fanny packs.

*seriously, call me if you ever need to talk: (512) 296-7080.*

*continued...*

Mary Ellen Massa, Ego's Bar in Austin, Jay for making the best Chocolate Choo-Choos, Lucius for being the best slam doorman, Phil and Michelle West, Mike Henry and Sonya Feher, David Hendler (thanks for help with the cover!), Andy Buck, Tony Jackson, Michael P. Whalen, Lynn Mykeska, Ragan Fox, Sarah Quenon, Matthew John Conley, Marc Bamuthi Joseph, Ariana Waynes, Blair Wilson, John Freitas, Bear (now SunRay), Daphne Gottlieb, Cas McGee, Charles Ellik, Jamie Kennedy, Sonia Whittle, Nazelah Jamison, Bill Zischang, Nisa Ahmad, Etheridge Knight, Shawn Taylor, Morris Stegosaurus, Alix Olson, Jenny Malin, Karen Finneyfrock, Beth Lisick, Karryn Nagel, Darcy Harris, Mark Mazlow, Jay Walker, Jason Carney, Cas McGee, Ill Skillz, Chris Branch, Peter of the Earth, Katy Asson, Jason Edwards and Thom and Bill, Ernie Cline and Susan B. Anthony Somers-Willet, Alyssa Weller, Shappy and Cristin O'Keefe Aptowitz, Guy LeCharles Gonzalez, Amye Wilson, Stephanie Stone, Aimy Steadman, Annie La Ganga, Christopher Watson, McNichol and May, Erin Livingstone, Rialistic, Kealoha, Leslie Moniot, Lynne Procope, Roger Bonair-Agard, Nick Fox, Christopher Fox Graham, Lob, Mark Schaffer, Dayvid Figler, Ben Ortiz, Amalia Ortiz, Shaggy, Poetri, Shihan, Ben Porter Lewis, Rachel Kahn, G. Murray Thomas, Victor Infante and Leah Duschenes, the OKC crew (Lydia, Taz, Tapestry, Boston Bridgewater, Spontaneous Bob, etc.), Nicki Miller, Denise Johnson, Gabrielle Boulliane, Linda Stehling, Leigh Rae Griffin, Loudgirl, Katy Domogala, Alexandra Darch Stolarski, Walidah Imarisha, Jennifer Braunstein from Scholastic Press, Panika Dillon, Shelja Patel, Andy Hall, David Huang, Vandy Ham, Vadim Litvak, Greg Gillam, Isangmahal, Genevieve van Cleve, Tara Hardy, Liz Wasson, Ethan Benda, Cat Tyc, Mindi Nettifee, Bowerbird Intelligentleman, Claudia Sherman, Cass King, Ms. Spelt, James Cagney, Jane Siberry, Justin Chin, Kelly McNally, Juliette Torrez, Kenn Rodriguez, Esther Griego, Danny Solis, Gary Glazner, Kelly Suzanne Woods, Jim Nave, Jose Guveia, Elise Winters-Huete, Esteban Hinojosa, Brenda Moossy, John Powers, Kim Jordan, Tamera Slayton, Aaron Trumm, Kyria Abrahams, Michael Brown, April Ardito, Henry Sampson, Steve and Deb Marsh, Mark Sweet, Sammi Mora, Jeffrey McDaniel, Gayle Danley, Al Letson, Hilary Thomas, Linzee Holmes, Nandi Crosby, Mark Robison, Paul Devlin, Faith Huete, Tracey Smith, Omolara, Jeff Knight, Larry Jaffe, Bill and Sue MacMillan, Tarin Towers, Kristen Carey, Thea Hillman, Sarah Oleksyk, Sander and Nick formerly at Soft Skull, Michelle and Sini from Sister Spit, Kristal Ashe, Eitan Kadosh, Buddy Wakefield, Gregory Hischak, Felice Bell, E-Go, Charles Ardinger, Robert Carroll, Jerry Quickley, Rick Lupert, Taylor Mali, Beau Sia, Saul Williams, Al Letson, Aya De Leon, Markus Rene Van, Hoonmin Jung (who makes the best burgers ever!), Bob Holman, Patricia Smith, Dan Houston, Garland Thompson, James Kass, Jeff and Karen Kass, Jen O'Hare and her mom Linda and her sister Lindsay, Shannon Williams, Herb Hughes and Shannon Rooney and Nancy Talley and Chloe Cook and all the Chico Crew from way back, every person who has ever given me a featured reading at their venue or a couch to sleep on in their apartment, everyone who has ever dated me or made love to me or kissed me or held me tight and spooned me or simply looked deeply in my eyes and made me sigh, and most of all to you, whoever you are, for holding this book in your hand and reading the words out loud. It means everything to me. The core problem with a list like this is that it will never truly be finished. I will expand it forever. I love you like the whole world and miss you very much. If you're not here and know you should be, let me know, and I'll correct my mistake of omission. BPE. June 15, 2007 at 11:30 p.m. *Amelie* soundtrack. Chilling with Zara & cats. Peace.

*i mean, don't call at 3 a.m., but call me.*

**BIG POPPA E** is a spoken word artist and three-time HBO *Def Poet* who melds rhythmic verse, stand-up comedy, and dramatic monologue into explosive works that skewer pop culture, politics, and the pain and beauty of relationships. His musings have led to appearances on BET's *The Way We Do It* sketch comedy series, National Public Radio, and CBS's *60 Minutes* (although, truth be told, he was only on for about three seconds... but still...) Recently, his viral video *Why I Got Fired From Apple Computer* was viewed over a million times on sites across the Internet, including YouTube and Google Video, garnering links from hundreds of websites.

Big Poppa E burst onto the scene as a member of the '99 San Francisco Poetry Slam Team, co-champions of the '99 National Poetry Slam in Chicago and the only undefeated team out of 48 that year. The piece he performed on the finals stage — *¡The Wussy Boy Manifesto!* — has since become a rallying cry for outcasts, dorks, dweebs, and feebs everywhere, leading *Ms. Magazine* to proclaim him "an icon for effeminate males" and *The Los Angeles Times* to declare him "the leader of the new Wussy Boy movement." The piece is now one of the most popular slam works performed by high school and college speech competitors across the country.

Big Poppa E has toured relentlessly on the spoken word highway since 2000, when he did 65 gigs across 27 states in just under four months. In the summer of 2003 alone, he logged over 21,000 miles on his '99 Ford Windstar mini-van, which has since been retired after 200,000 miles. He has headlined at more than 70 universities and colleges and performed 150+ poetry slam features in 40 states (including Hawaii and Alaska). Along the way, his tours have generated over a hundred stories in newspapers and magazines in the US, Canada, England, and Australia, including such publications as: *The New York Times; The Washington Post; The Ottowa Citizen; The London Daily Express; The Sydney Morning Herald; Bust Magazine; Poets and Writers;* and *The Utne Reader.*

Big Poppa E is the author of six books of poetry, two collections of haiku, two CDs, two DVDs, and a bunch of T-shirts and stickers. He has been published in *Poetry Slam: The Competitive Art of Performance Poetry* on Manic D Press, and his essay *Slam Your Way Across America* was included in the *Poets and Writers* magazine collection *The Practical Writer: From Inspiration to Publication.* He has two tuxedo kitties named Aretha and Thelonious. He currently calls Austin, Texas, his home and serves as DJ Hot Wings every week at the Austin Poetry Slam.

*thank you.*

Printed in the United States
86877LV00006B/213/A